"A near-death experience that inspires beyond imagination!

"In . . . *The Half-Known Life*, we find highly inspiring and motivating quotes from well-known people. The author himself provides the same in the titles of his chapters, such as 'Becoming You: Your Relationship with Yourself.' Another chapter is entitled, 'Your Relationship with the World.' He continues to highlight 'Lessons from Near-Death.'

"Another commonality between us is that each of our near-death experiences impacts how we live life, all for the better. Should you desire to know more and find inspiration packed with motivation, I highly recommend his book!"

—Elinor Stutz, author of *Nice Girls DO Get the Sale: Relationship Building That Gets Results*, and *HIRED!: How to Use Sales Techniques to Sell Yourself on Interviews*

"As Ryan says in this book, truly profound change happens following events that shake you to your core. Fortunately, we have gifted people like Ryan who can share such experiences and life lessons so that we can change without them. Life will always demand something significant from us. Ryan shows us how to deliver with excellence!"

—Ben Woodward, author of *The Empowerment Paradox: Seven Vital Virtues to Turn Struggle Into Strength*

"The back cover of this book states that *The Half-Known Life* will 'challenge conventional thinking of success, identity and personal change.' I come away with a slightly different, but related, viewpoint. The author's story challenges human thinking in general, and offers a shift in attitude and perception of this kind of thinking that can lead to great transformation, not just 'personal change.' Without relying on religious, metaphysical, scientific, or even spiritual prompts, Ryan approached his readers, instead, with solid common sense blanketed in a poetry of words, scenarios, and explanations that resonate at the most basic level. We are so much more than we think we are!

"I recommend this book for anyone who has the courage to change. It will prove to be of particular benefit to those who shy away from more orchestrated cosmologies. Pay attention to the arguments for thinking and doing things from a fresh new attitude and perspective. Ryan shows how it is from the level of 'elevated' common sense and the changes that come with it that the potential and opportunity to change our lives once and for all can be delivered."

—Linda Kolsky, author of *Heavenly Hindsights: How One Mother Found Meaning in Life After the Death of Her Child*

"*The Half-Known Life* offers an insightful look into the very busy world we all live in. It encourages us to rethink what is important and provides thoughtful commentary on ways to make our lives more meaningful in the moment. Thought-provoking questions help the reader dig deep into the motives behind our feelings and actions. An engaging and relatable read that will leave you reassessing life's priorities."

—Simone Yemm, author of *Stalked By Demons, Guarded By Angels*

"*The Half-Known Life* is a gift to your soul. Reading this book will not only entertain you but give you a profound sense of how to live a full life, with all the struggles that the universe throws at you. Identity, self-love, and self-mastery are just a few of the themes that Ryan tackles with grace and humor."

—Andy Chaleff, author of *The Wounded Healer*

*The Half-Known Life:*
*What Matters Most When You're Running Out of Time*

by Ryan Lindner

© Copyright 2022 Ryan Lindner

ISBN 978-1-64663-645-7

Published by

**köehlerbooks**™

3705 Shore Drive
Virginia Beach, VA 23455
800-435-4811
www.koehlerbooks.com

# the half-known life

### what matters most when you're running out of time

## ryan lindner

VIRGINIA BEACH
CAPE CHARLES

*If you want to be a grocer, or a general, or a politician, or a judge, you will invariably become it; that is your punishment. If you never know what you want to be, if you live what some might call the dynamic life but what I will call the artistic life, if each day you are unsure of who you are and what you know, you will never become anything, and that is your reward.*

**—OSCAR WILDE**

# Walking the Tightrope

It was the day everything went black.

"I'm going down now," I said to a young woman a few seconds before the darkness—my first cardiac arrest. I knew it was coming, even if only for a few seconds. What I didn't realize was that I was just beginning a years-long journey whereby through near-constant dizziness and fatigue—the ebbs and flows of a myriad of strange symptoms—I would come face-to-face with the clock of life that's wound but once.

We all have this clock, but I can always hear its tick, the ever-present reminder to manage my energy as I walk the tightrope, always a misstep away from falling into my dark world again.

When I opened my eyes after my second cardiac arrest, less than a day after the first, a ring of doctors and nurses encircled my hospital bed. Stroking my forehead, a nurse softly comforted me. "You're okay," she whispered. I still see flashes of her face.

What happened to me was a big mystery, it seemed, and in the days and weeks that followed, I tried to make sense of it. I had a random, unexplained cardiac event, and this strange mechanical device in my chest not much larger than a silver dollar was now supposed to keep me alive.

"It's my first step toward becoming a cyborg," I often joked. But it was hard to trust this small, battery-operated lump bulging from my chest under another scar.

Lying in the hospital bed, I pictured my life years ago—the struggle: My shirt was filthy and smelled of the pizza sauce that painted it from collar to tail. Working any job I could get, I often found myself working into the night, waiting tables, delivering pizzas, and sustaining myself on old, discarded breadsticks I'd eat in my car. My shoes were held on with duct tape, although it never kept my socks from becoming soaked in the rain. *That* situation seemed so hopeless. *Is this all my life is?* I'd think. *Is this all I am?* I held back tears.

But after years of what seemed like a never-ending nightmare, I emerged on the other side—the side of success—and landed what I would've once called my "dream job."

Things seemed to finally be going well . . . until they weren't—until the darkness came.

I sat in the hospital bed after the darkness, each breath a reminder that, yes, I was alive. For how long, no one could tell. I struggled to process the gravity of what had just happened.

I had no personal or family history of heart problems. I was young and a former collegiate athlete who ate what most would call obsessively, even annoyingly "clean." I consumed a mostly plant-based diet, was a nonsmoker, and for many years I logged my sleep.

As a behavioral coach, personal development specialist, and trainer helping many people shift toward new perspectives and life changes in order to become well, I was dedicated to that same wellness. So it was especially hard to grasp why I suddenly became the youngest of my doctor's patients with a pacemaker.

For most people, especially the young, mortality is a foggy, distant idea. *This* wasn't supposed to happen. But it did. One moment I was fine, and the next, I was a crumpled mass on the floor, a shell—a sum total of a network of blood vessels, neurons, and chemicals that were all once part of a person. Was I more than that?

Sometimes I think of the stories of young athletes who just drop dead one day at football practice in the August heat. "That's me," I said as I tried to explain things to so many curious people. I had questions, too. I was *that* guy, except I had the right people around to help at precisely the right time.

Only moments earlier, I had been driving. What would I have done *then*?

I've always appreciated the simpler times of the past, without all the noise. I'm often captivated by antiques, imagining the story behind something created when things weren't so commercialized; there was more beauty. Sometimes I even joke that perhaps I was born at the wrong time. But at any other time, without all the medical advances— the pacemakers, defibrillators, and all the other makings of a cyborg— I'd be dead.

"What if you were alone?" people sometimes ask.

"What happened?! Did you see a white light?"

"No," I answer, disappointedly. "But it was hot and smelled a bit like sulfur . . ."

I knew little about what caused the event necessitating my pacemaker, and I struggled to make sense of my life in all the familiar ways—a life that seemed to be suddenly, wildly spinning out of control, and in which now so much felt empty.

The dizziness is the hardest to explain. I mean, how do you describe the color blue? There aren't words to describe some things. But I sometimes feel like my head's in a vise, underwater. There's weakness in my extremities as if I'm not quite in control. There's also extreme fatigue that no amount of sleep mitigates.

Then there's the teetering on the edge of consciousness. With one foot in this world and another foot in the darkness, I become clammy, light-headed, and my vision blurs as the fringes of my field of view close. And, yes, I've seen all the specialists—the best. But all I can do is treat symptoms; the cause is a mystery.

The worst thing is the moment the darkness comes, when it closes in: that terrifying moment and the utter loss of control, knowing there's not a damn thing I can do—the horror of living moment to moment thinking it's your last, thinking it's all happening again and again and that it never stops. *That's* where I live, waiting for the dormant, the darkness, the monster that awaits.

After my two cardiac arrests, with no paid time off and in dire financial need, I chose to return to work against my doctor's orders. And a few days after leaving the ICU, I was back at the office.

I've had thousands of clients, including members of all four military branches—physicians, psychologists, business executives, and even organizations. I helped them explore ways to shift within themselves, to maximize their time and transform aspects of their lives they were too busy to live. I helped them through change—change in career, relationship, health, and habits.

Everything seemed different after the darkness.

As I returned to work, it became maddening to hear, for the ten thousandth time, about all-consuming everyday problems and misguided priorities. I fought to remain conscious while I listened to the thralls of bathroom remodels and kids' soccer practices, the trivial work gossip, or complaints of afternoon traffic.

"How are things going this week? Were you able to try what we talked about? I know you mentioned setting some time aside after your son's nap to put your resume draft together," I said to Susan, one of my regular clients who was working to develop healthier habits and transition to another career.

"I did a lot of thinking about it, for sure, but I was busy with the laundry, and then I got a call from work. I'll start tomorrow."

*Sure you will,* I thought as she started along another tangent before I reeled her back in. *And how will tomorrow be different? Or less busy?*

Indeed, Susan was busy, exhausted, and overwhelmed from managing a household with three boys under the age of ten and a husband frequently away for work. She spoke in circles, more a cathartic venting than anything else, the same stories repeating themselves for years before we met. She could never quite catch up with all she had to do, never able to get her head above water. She wanted to change, but the things she did never amounted to anything truly lasting.

I pictured a hamster running around her wheel, waiting for a change in circumstance around the corner, certain that the busyness was something that happened *to* her. Each opportunity to change was too inconvenient, and every circumstance a crisis. Like many people, she was not quite able to gain traction, constantly frazzled and on the edge of sanity.

Susan's path to a solution seemed so clear *to me,* but she wasn't ready. As most people tend to do, she handled my dozens of suggestions in one specific way: she could only see the reasons why they wouldn't work. Something became clear—a realization I would take with me for the rest of my career. People don't change unless they choose change; they don't like to be sold. You can't convince anyone of anything. They have to come to their own conclusions. Even if the idea is from elsewhere, they have to decide to be open to it.

When we're stuck, we can only see the reasons why something won't work, no matter how clear the path seems to others. On many occasions, upon hearing how overwhelmed a client was, I would privately marvel that the solution seemed to be right in front of them, but they couldn't see it.

Most "problems" are first-world problems; they always look different from the outside. As frustrating as traffic is, there are people in the world struggling to find clean water. And, as with any problem, all sorts of avenues for change regularly present themselves, but most people can't see them. It doesn't matter how smart you are. As I saw with psychologists, physicians, counselors, executives, and generals as clients, you can help others all day but still not see yourself.

Susan's experience is not unlike so many others. Like a black hole, the busyness sucks you in, stealing from you, robbing you of the opportunity to live as you really are and see life with all its beauty. Instead, you're trudging through the endless to-do list, head down, lost in the weeds. And then one day it's over, the to-do list left undone.

Most often, truly profound change happens following events that shake you to your core—a car accident, death of a family member, or cardiac arrest—and pull you into a moment of clarity. Priorities change when time becomes precious. Problems look different when you have no energy left to give them. After all, marathon runners don't say much on mile twenty; they choose to breathe. And all I have to give is channeled into each moment that I'm awake. I, too, choose to breathe.

The less energy you have, the more aware of it you are—the energy you always gave away so freely. You spent it like currency. Energy *is* currency. Time is currency—*time currency*. And each moment is a conscious choice of expenditure. I don't have the luxury of overdrawing. I've borrowed too much and can no longer push through the busyness, lest my condition worsen and the darkness comes again.

I remember once standing in an airport, my feet like anvils. I could only throw my dead weight forward one leg at a time; there was such heaviness there—a strange weakness that's difficult to describe. But it's terrifying. Alone, I felt the loss of control as I grew light-headed and clammy. Every step, every breath, was an all-encompassing effort. With each moment, I was grateful I was still conscious as I staggered through the hustle and bustle—the hundreds of busy people in a hurry, on their phones, with schedules to keep.

It can be a solitary road. No one knows quite how you feel. They can't. And you can't describe it, which doesn't make it easier. Doctors don't always seem to believe you, especially those who are used to the familiar diagnoses, like the flu. You know they're thinking it must all be in your head. It's hard for people to understand when you don't always look "sick."

"Push it too hard? Maybe you didn't hydrate enough," said a passerby at the gym on one of those light-headed days as I lay sprawled out on a locker room bench, terrified.

"Thanks," I said. *You have no idea.* I was always afraid of creating a scene.

"Do you want me to stay with you?" an older man who looked long retired said as he closed his locker and picked up his gym bag.

"No thanks. I'm good," I said, which wasn't true. *Just make it through*, I thought. But in those situations, you don't take for granted the slightest offer of help. Or comfort. I felt like a scared little kid.

It was extraordinarily difficult to return to work. After all, you don't appreciate not being sick until you are. You don't appreciate not having a migraine until you do. You don't appreciate not seeing your loved ones until they're gone.

Most workplaces, especially the large, stuffy corporate ones, felt empty—empty relationships, or at least few that ventured beyond hallway pleasantries; empty tasks; empty purpose; and bereft of humanity as people are reduced to roles. If, for example, you lost your job tomorrow, they'd replace you in a millisecond. No one there hears the clock's tick, but I do. And they will, too, one day.

I wish I could say my brushes with death catalyzed a major mental shift, but mostly I thought along these lines with some varying degree of awareness. But now the fleeting nature of life is all I think about, my attention continuously pulled into every moment in ways that once only existed in my periphery. Indeed, living with the constant fear of death makes you truly appreciate how much of a gift you have here.

On one particular day, during another terrifying struggle to stay conscious, I attended a birthday luncheon for a work colleague at a local restaurant. I ordered two bowls of high-sodium soup and chugged as much water as I could hold to keep my blood pressure high enough to stay conscious. I received a few strange looks regarding my odd taste, but no one could guess what it was like in my lonely world. These aren't uncommon strategies to remain upright lest I slump over in a pool of sweat, the paramedics carting me out of the office on a stretcher, which has happened. I was smiling one moment and slumped over the next. When do you call for help when you always feel that way? I've seen world-renowned specialists. I've run the gamut of medications. I've learned to manage symptoms, not causes.

"I just saw Ryan in the hall; he seemed okay . . ." I heard a colleague say as the paramedics did what they did. My smile just moments earlier had been a facade. My forehead on the desk, I heard the rumblings around me. I hated making a scene, but all you can do is think about one breath, then another, and then another.

I call each of these events a "crash": a relapse into an almost unbearable barrage of symptoms, after which I begin to pick up the pieces of my life as I feel better, although never quite "normal"—just normal *for me*. I was always about a foot away from my blood pressure cuff and, initially, a heart monitor. Often taking clients over the phone or video, it was easy to hide these things.

The basic patterns of clients were these: First, they always thought their busyness was unique to them, unaware that it's a collective problem. Second, they lived to complete their to-do lists, with a seemingly endless supply of tomorrows upon which relief awaited. And third, they were blind to the ways they perpetuated their predicament, each moment merely a reaction to the last.

Everyone wants the perfect formula to stick to personal change, and there is no shortage of self-help books professing the best method to save time or find that elusive success they spend so much time chasing (and which is never enough). Perhaps they've "read all the books." *They just aren't doing it.*

If you clean out a hoarder's home, you've changed the home. You've treated a symptom. And if you only focus on treating the symptom, you'll never reach the cause. In other words, what about a person's approach to their own life created that issue in the first place?

If you tell a messy person, "This is how I think you should stay clean and organized," it might make sense to them, but there's often something inherent in them that has created that situation, and it'll be a mess again in a week. A busy person will always stay busy because *they're a busy person.* It has more to do with them than with their to-do list. They think life is just happening *to* them, a victim of circumstances they believe are unique.

Plus, if you talk to ten different people, they're going to have ten different ways of staying organized and managing their time that works (or doesn't work) for them to varying degrees. And they're all quick to provide advice about what you should do. But again, people don't want to be sold. They have to come to it on their own.

Many "experts" are quick to tell you what's going to work as if there were a "right" way to do something—their own branded remedy for the stress, or a "revolutionary" path to success. What they're telling you is their opinion about what works for them in their situation. It may be good advice, or not. Again, ask ten experts what works, and you'll hear ten different opinions, some of which you've heard and will struggle to apply in daily life.

*The Half-Known Life* challenges conventional thinking about success, identity, and personal change. It can help remove blind spots that keep you from seeing what matters most as you're entranced by the to-do list that never seems to end—a life on autopilot. It's not a sunshine-and-rainbows book. It's about what's real and exploring answers to the right questions, perhaps allowing you a different life perspective and helping you to take the first step toward change.

Only when pulled into the present moment by a trauma, a life-changing experience that rocks them to their core, or on their deathbed do most people see life so clearly. And they reflect: What's their time worth? What are their relationships worth? their opinions? their problems? their worries? their dramas? their roles? their accolades? their possessions? their stress? How much of that was unnecessary or self-created without their knowing? What was *real*?

No single program or guru can fix your life. There's no tip that isn't just an opinion or experience. With promises of boundless success, many gurus focus on the chase—on becoming this person you've created in your head who will make you complete, provided you follow the guru's magical tips. But self-awareness, or *life*-awareness, is one thing no one can give you and money can't buy.

Life is made up of countless tiny microdecisions about what is and isn't worth your energy. We think we know what matters but choose other things. We also know to eat healthily, sleep well, and drink little. But we don't. We put it off, get distracted, or become paralyzed when attempting change.

It will take more than a vacation, massage, yoga, or an organizational book to transform your life. And no amount of getting organized, color-coding your files, or expert tips are going to change your relationship with the one thing you can't get back: time.

If, one year from now, your life is exactly the same, how will you feel? What was fundamentally different one year ago? Don't wait until you're burnt out or you experience a life-changing event to get real about your life. Who are you when all of the accolades and accomplishments are gone? You can master time management, but what does how you manage that time say about what's important to you—about what matters most?

We might think we are lawyers or accountants or clerks or landscapers, but really, we are time traders. We give our time, usually for something cheap in return. Remember, if something doesn't add to your life, it takes away. And time always seems slow in the moment. One day you'll realize that it quietly vanished without your knowing.

Don't be a bystander. Get out of your head and get into your life before it slips away.

*Consider the subtleness of the sea; how its most dreaded creatures glide under water, unapparent for the most part, and treacherously hidden beneath the loveliest tints of azure. . . . For as this appalling ocean surrounds the verdant land, so in the soul of man there lies one insular Tahiti, full of peace and joy, but encompassed by all the horrors of the half-known life.*

**—HERMAN MELVILLE**

CHAPTER ONE

# Daily Life:

## *Living for Weekends*

❖

**Lessons from Near Death:**

*There's no such thing as "work life" or "personal life." There's just life. Stop wishing it away as you wait for a better tomorrow that never comes.*

❖

"How are you?" the barista asked the woman in front of me as I waited.

"Good, you?" she said quickly before ordering.

My turn.

"How are you?" the barista asked.

I felt a strange, visceral recoil at the question, which wasn't a real question at all.

"Fantastic, thank you," I said. It wasn't a real answer.

We are asked this question all day, every day—at the checkout counter, getting coffee, and in the hallway at work. It's like a handshake, a greeting, a pleasantry, but every time someone asks, I can't help but cringe. Again, it's not a real question, and no one expects a real answer.

"How are you?" a coworker asked another in the breakroom. It was the third time I'd heard the question in half an hour.

"Good, and you?" she replied, except that she wasn't. I knew Cathy, and she was in the middle of a messy divorce, was an alcoholic, and was about to engage in a lengthy court battle over property, child visitation, and more. But at work, we're taught that you're not *that* person. You're the perception others have of you, which is a sum of roles.

You're a role at home, too. You're a parent, or child, or brother, or caretaker, or spouse. With each role comes the responsibility of all the things you have to do. Soon, your entire life is consumed by these things, and the best you can do is keep trudging through. So, you're not "good." You're busy.

The noise is all around you. It's deafening. You brush your teeth, feed the dog, rush to get the kids ready, fight traffic, check a hundred emails, deal with work drama, and make three appointments, all by noon.

For lunch, if you're lucky enough for an actual break, you'll chat with a colleague about a coworker who isn't pulling their weight. You'll talk about what you saw on television or your plans for the weekend. You'll debate whether to confront the slacker about their lack of productivity in the department; it's annoying that management can't see you're carrying them. It's a rough day, and the week just started. But it's Monday, after all.

All your conversations on a Monday are about the fact it's a Monday. You remind everyone, and when making small talk, when someone asks how you are, you blame Monday for the tepid response. You're already worried about getting ahead of schedule so you can pick up the kids from their half day at school, which throws a wrench into things. This feeling of perpetual discomfort is familiar. It's daily. It's normal. You think that if you get through this or that, somehow there will be an end to the stress. Even if you intellectually know this is not true, you try to believe that this stress is circumstantial, just for this situation. But it never is.

People sometimes assume that work is separate from life and so does not encompass the humanity that "real life" does. But there's no "work life" or "personal life"; there's just life. Your "work" is an extension of your life.

Your experience of life is often an uncomfortable, stressful one, a series of mental and emotional reactions. These reactions are narrated by a voice in your head—an incessant mental commentary you think is who you are. But this commentary is not you; it's the series of reactions. You react to something, and then you react to the reaction.

Most of life is this automatic cycle of knee-jerk reactions. You feel something and automatically react. The busier you become, the more automatic. You're so busy that your lack of time and energy makes what does not require presence (i.e. what is familiar) an easier choice because it requires less energy. You're spread thin and never seem to have enough energy to be fully "here" as your attention and accompanying dialogue is somewhere ahead of you and down the to-do list.

"Stress is normal," many experts say. This is true, but "stress" is a broad term, and we speak as if it's something of which we're victims—something that controls us without our permission. Most "experts" don't know any different because they can't know any different. They can't see beyond their own experience.

Stress, however, is a feeling, a reaction to a situation. Reactions become habits that we chalk up to the circumstances. "That's life," we say. It's a routine series of tasks, one after the other, again and again. While we can cope with a certain amount of stress as a series of daily peaks and valleys, we are unable to cope with the stress as a constant peak. Imagine the experience of stress as waves on an electrocardiogram, each peak or increase in stress followed by a recovery, or valley. Over time, peaks and valleys spike closer together; they swell to the point where you can't distinguish between one peak and the next. On an electrocardiogram, it looks like one solid, unchanging flat line—the flatline of your life.

Stressors you may otherwise be able to handle individually are more difficult because without the possibility of recouping energy for reflection, rest, or processing, you simply don't have enough energy left in the tank to live in a meaningful way. Any energy left is diverted to coping for the stress, the discomfort, or the emptiness—whatever feels good right now, whatever distracts you now.

Habits require less energy because, over time, you're wired that way. And for that reason, change in your life is unlikely. You're reactive from one moment to the next, and you never feel quite "like yourself." You may want change but don't have the energy to do anything about it. The familiar is more convenient, so you stick to that.

In other words, you never have a recovery from stress, so you're reactive, and your reactivity only drives more reactivity. And you can't see the big picture of your life. You have blind spots. The constant tension reduces immune-system function and increases the likelihood of illness—mental and physical. So you feel worse. And when you feel worse, you do more things that make you worse.

Of course, different people will respond differently to stress— take introverts and extroverts, for example. Although they recover differently, their relative stress, the busyness, is equally cumulative.

You say something to your boss about a conflict with your colleague. Long after the incident, your mind still goes over and over it and engages in an exhausting internal dialogue about the incident. A week later, you're still rewatching the movie in your mind, which is noisy. So, not only are you physically busy, but you're mentally busy, too.

The past always primes the future. One moment defines the next because you obsessively hold the emotional remnants of the past. Thus, you're always living in the past in the form of pain or the future in the form of anxiety conditioned by that past.

How you think about change also keeps you stuck. Each thought leads to an emotional reaction, and this reaction leads to a behavior. If you don't feel good about change, your behaviors never create it. Then your thoughts become self-fulfilling prophecies as you confirm what you already thought: that it wouldn't work. Your future is shaped by the constant search for confirmation that what you believe is true. If what you believe about your life isn't true, then how do you know what is? That's the question that drives many people to dangerous methods of coping for an emptiness they don't understand.

So you go back to what's familiar and automatic and stressful: the routine. At least then you feel relative control over your life and your place in it. But you don't eat well, sleep well, and there's something missing. Your mind becomes obsessed with reconciliation of events from the past that make no difference to the present and, relative to who you are, never made any difference.

Most people live this way for years, decades, or lifetimes; all the while, they have no idea. If they did, no one would choose the pain, stress, or emptiness. Instead, they're victims of circumstance.

To put this another way, let's go back to the statement "Stress is normal," meaning you can't get rid of stress. That's true because it's true to you. But the stress I'm referring to is the constant, unnecessary stress that comprises the bulk of our life experience. You've made what you understand to be necessary stress normal. But rather than looking at a situation, responding, and moving on, you carry it with mental commentaries that have you stuck in the mind-numbing analysis of things that don't matter and situations outside your control.

Reactions are your mind's attempt to control outcomes—the ego's trick to steer situations in its favor. Were you ever party to an argument that seemed to escalate quickly, almost suddenly? Perhaps it escalated to the point where both parties forgot the original issue, instead finding themselves in a very different argument about something someone said or how they said it. In this way, each was trying to "one-up" the other so as not to feel diminished. Each moment a reaction to the last, you needed to "win" to avoid feeling lessened. Did that feel automatic to you? Almost as if that interaction were unavoidable, and you were powerless to stop it?

Emotions drive situations. People will almost always come up or down to your emotional level. If you react defensively, they will as well. Every action will lead to a proportional reaction. Each person triggers that defensiveness in the other because to reconcile their emotions, they have to make the other person less. Likewise, if you remain calm, they will soon join you. You can only yell at someone so long before realizing you're the only one yelling.

Next time you're in an argument, wait. Wait for the other person to finish venting. Then, you can speak to them more reasonably. If you trigger their defensiveness with defensiveness of your own, it will only escalate from there.

You felt slighted, disrespected, diminished by the other person. Did they "make" you feel that way? No. What in you was diminished, really? Nothing. It's in your head.

"Would you rather be right or be happy?" When's the last time that in explaining your rightness to an upset person, they suddenly agreed with you and then apologized? "You know what? You're right. I'm sorry." That seldom happens. A person can't see their own lives, behaviors, or thoughts if they're lost in them.

"I'm so sorry," you might say after a heated argument. "I don't know what got into me." Pain got into you—because what someone thinks makes a difference to who you are, to how you feel about yourself.

Reading this, you might say, "I don't care what other people think," but that's rarely true. That's something people say because they feel better, stronger saying it. It's armor.

When you feel constant pain, you cope both by seeking things that quickly soothe or numb that pain (food, alcohol, etc.) and by building perceptions of yourself (and your worth) through things you think add value—titles, accolades, clothes, cars, followers, associations, and relationships. This means collecting things that ostensibly make you more *you* because something is missing and you think you can find it in things.

Every day, you confirm who you are through others' reactions to you. Comments to your posts on social media, your clothes, car, etc., are all pieces of the puzzle of you that other people put together through their reactions. How else would you know who you are if not through others' reactions to you? And your mind tries to control those reactions through everything you do.

Much of your daily stress is a result of the degree of your perceived control, or lack thereof, of your personal value and the energy spent reconciling perceived discrepancies in that value. That, too, is in your head—as if personal value were something to be earned or you have to do something to be more "enough." The way we understand self-worth is a cultural pandemic shaped by everything outside of you that you let define you—things that mean nothing.

Humans are the only species that don't live in moments, and humans carry all the burdens of their internal dialogue. Consider these questions: Which beetle is better? Which blade of grass is better? Which street sign is better? You have no idea what to make of these comparisons because there's no measure to it; it's incomprehensible. The purpose of two beetles is to be alive; that's it. The purpose of a blade of grass is to exist. There's no value to be earned or had. Like the beetle or the blade of grass, your purpose is to be alive and experience your life.

Instead, we work, are exhausted, and add things to the to-do list quicker than we can complete them. Work is the center point of life. Your work, which is usually a job you most certainly wouldn't do unless you got paid for it, is "who you are," but you don't know what that means. You use it to "get ahead" and build what you think is your value. If you aren't "ahead," you must be "behind." You feel it.

You don't live life; it lives you.

*Life is the dancer and you are the dance.*

**—ECKHART TOLLE**

To feel better, you seek "work-life balance." You meditate and do some yoga on vacation. But even then, your mind races. You're next to your phone constantly and feel naked without it. You obsessively scroll through your social-media feed, keeping up with the world around you. You're only one day into vacation, and you can't help but think about all you have to do when you return.

The illusion is that stress is merely an effect of the busyness and all you need is a vacation. After all, there are only fifteen years to go until retirement (which is never what you hope it is).

In every interaction, you tell coworkers, "I'm hanging in there. It's been a crazy week," as if it were different than any other week. You act like the busy week is an anomaly, and you long for the weekend reprieve. Food, drink, sex, drugs, validation from social media, and other coping methods do little to help because they never treat a root cause of your discomfort. You feel better, briefly, because you're distracted. Then you feel worse. You feel a loss of control as if each release beckons you, taunts you.

You can't address the root cause because you can't see it. What is it you're distracting yourself from?

Anything you can't simply stop is an addiction of some sort. When we are addicted to something, like food, we wait (sometimes forever) until we fix all the things that need fixing in our lives that we think make us "ready" for that change. But you don't have to align your life to the stars to be ready to take the first step. Do it now, today, because waiting can last a lifetime. Today is where your choices live, in a thousand little microdecisions.

For a moment, picture a gauge of your mental energy (arousal) like the fuel gauge on your car. On one end of the spectrum is understimulation (or boredom), and on the other, overstimulation (being overwhelmed, depressed). The middle of the spectrum is complacency—a place where you're fully functional and have just enough energy to cope, to handle the busyness and make it through the day's tasks; you aren't quite happy or fulfilled, but you aren't in the deepest despair, either. Most people are somewhere in complacency, only occasionally drifting to one extreme or the other.

I often work with clients who are in discomfort (stress) and are either overwhelmed (too busy) or bored (aimless, purposeless). They experience life as a string of emotions linked to events that have already happened and over which they have no control; they hash these events ad nauseum to reconcile those emotions—to give themselves permission to feel okay about them.

Generally, you can deal with times of high stimulation, but you'll always require recovery. Those who don't recover sufficiently from these high-stimulation states seek soothing from some convenient yet fleeting daily source.

Then there's boredom. Instead of the anxiety associated with overstimulation, when bored you might experience withdrawal and feelings of isolation or aimlessness.

Most people look for happiness on this scale. But you're always a circumstance away from crumbling. If life lives *you*, the victim of circumstance, you'll never be at peace. Happiness is a state of mind—an emotion. Peace is not. When you're at peace, you live in the moments. Life flows, and suddenly you're no longer a bystander.

Rewiring what's automatic is going to take some time. It starts with small things—like brushing your teeth, getting dressed, driving to work—when you can be present instead of trapped in the internal dialogue. Each task is in sync with you. You're there, in the task. You're in complete focus, like when a painter, chef, or mechanic is fully immersed in his or her work—when you lift your head and realize it's the end of a day that was fully lived, invested in each moment.

Having goals does not make you focused. Goals may be good to have so long as you know what's driving them. Otherwise, goals are just more of the same—endless tasks for better tomorrows and a more complete "you." Sure, create goals, but don't allow them to take you away from being present, and don't get attached to them as a reflection of who you are.

Consider New Year's resolutions. These are twisted goals people decide upon not because they're ready but out of obligation that they *should* have a goal because it's time to and everyone else is doing it. Their strategy for accomplishing such a goal is to simply "try," which is meaningless. They soon give up and fall back to what's familiar. They get "busy."

I once asked a client with two hyper young children, a full-time job, and a household to manage whether she was in the same place in her life, generally speaking, as she was five years ago. After a long pause, she quietly muttered, "Yes, yes I am."

Sure, titles, cars, addresses, or even the weight on the scale changes, but the essence of daily experience never does. And it never will. *You* change. Decisions change. And in order to change, you must understand how you think about change. Most people never get to a place where they can zoom out and get a clear, unobstructed view of their own lives and what it's actually going to take to create change. They don't know that they're not doing that. Most people can't slow down enough to take a real, honest look at themselves. They only ever catch a glimpse, flashes of reflection caused by some catalyst, such as when trauma or a near-death experience forces a pause. You have no problems in the ICU (except that you're in the ICU); you're in the moment.

The funny thing about being sick is that all your energy normally spent in daily doings gets siphoned into recovery. It's why people rarely change until they hit rock bottom. When they're feeling good, there's nothing to pull them into awareness. For a drug addict, "rock bottom"— the loss of jobs, money, relationships, or health, for example—usually has to happen before they get real. Sometimes it takes seeing the carnage of what was once used to ease pain but eventually destroyed their lives.

> *Almost all spiritual advances are preceded*
> *by a fall of some sort.*
>
> **—WAYNE DYER**

Change takes courage. Change requires decisive use of energy that comes from self-love. How can you help someone you don't care about? With every thought and action, you proclaim to the universe that *this* is worth the cost—in time, in energy. You never get it back, and you're its guardian.

Imagine that an overworked, stressed office worker, Michael, is jealous of his coworker Jan. Jan was recently recognized for her hard work and promoted as a result, although Michael perceives himself as a harder worker. Whether or not Michael gets credit, what does that change about what actually happened? Nothing. What changes? Perceptions do.

Michael feels diminished because he thinks *he's* the one that should be recognized; he's more deserving. And because his coworker received "his" recognition, Michael sees that as proof that others view him as less hardworking than Jan. So what really bothers him is that people are wrong about their perceptions of his value compared to Jan's value.

In his situation, perhaps you'd want to right this wrong and bring it to someone's attention, giving them a "piece of your mind" and bringing with you a mountain of evidence as you lament the unfairness of it all. But did you work hard for the sake of working hard, or did you work hard for the outcome you expected? If the latter is true, you'll always chase the dangling carrot, obsessing over things beyond your control, only happy when the stars align. If the former is true, recognition never factored into it.

So starts the internal dialogue. Most people, like Michael, play the mental movie of those events over and over again. *I worked so hard and did a ton of overtime! She doesn't deserve it. Hell, she never gets her reports right, anyway. Who does she think she is?* On and on Michael goes, replaying all the times Jan fell short. Or the time he covered for her when she was sick. Resentment builds.

Who made Michael feel this way? Michael did. His bitterness is like a splinter distracting him.

Michael has two choices, and only ever two. He will accept what has happened, or he will not; those are the choices. Without acceptance, you, like Michael, experience feelings of resistance. You disagree with the situation. You then become compelled to manipulate the situation in your favor by arguing your no-doubt valid points *that mostly make no difference in your life.* If you don't want a problem, don't create a problem.

Suppose Michael's boss acquiesces to appease a very angry Michael, and promotes him. It's not enough if it's lip service. Michael wants his boss to believe it. What he really wants isn't the recognition or the promotion but the knowing that he's "someone" in the eyes of others, which affects how Michael perceives himself.

This is not to say that anything goes or it's okay to allow yourself to be taken advantage of. Yes, there are times when you must speak up when something is wrong. But it's important to understand where it's coming from. What do you have to gain? Is it worth the energy? Would correcting this mistake make the truth truer? What difference does doing *this* actually make? Plus, all sorts of factors might be at play that you don't realize, none of which are worth your time. But if you do speak, do so without all the emotional underpinnings that define most reactions.

Most situations we encounter make no difference to who we are. Most time is spent on things out of our control. Again, you can't convince anyone of anything. No matter how reasonable you are, they have to choose it.

The question is, how much time do you, or Michael, want to put into this? Will it mean anything? No, it won't, and you've wasted all your mental energy for a week thinking about it. Congratulations. Feel better?

The truth is often lost in translation. One person perceives something, and the other perceives another. Both are right and neither are; the truth is somewhere between.

Whenever I hear about a situation or a problem like Michael's, I always remember that I hear only half a story, and it's different when you ask the other person—like asking Michael's coworker Jan. It's all perception.

When your mind becomes noisy, you'll never hear the clock's tick. Time management is like poker. With each life choice, you wager your bets, a lot or a few, and so profess, "Yes, *this* is worth the cost."

# CHAPTER TWO

# Interactions or Transactions:

## *Your Relationship with Other People*

❖

**Lessons from Near Death:**

*Most people aren't used to real interactions; they're profoundly rare. They're used to being a means to an end. You never know the impact you can have on someone simply by being fully present with them in the moment.*

❖

"I'm basically happy," some will say. But what they mean is that they experience flashes of situational happiness sprinkled into a mostly uncomfortable daily experience in which they're bystanders.

The moment you arrive at work, you long for the day's or week's end. Every moment outside of work is spent thinking of all you still have to do. For most people, the last thing they do before bed and the first thing they do after waking is in front of a screen.

You're only half there. By the time you get to one moment, you're already thinking about the next.

Thursday evening, you feel great. One more day to go! Now it's Friday. Congratulations, you "made it." After work, the weekend clock starts. Now you can live. The trouble is, you're exhausted, so you plop on the couch with a bottle of wine. Saturday races by, and you feel it slipping away. You feel nagging anxiety—a reminder that you'd planned to "live it up" today while you could, but it's getting late.

Sunday morning comes, and it starts—the real dread. The weekend nights are gone, and Sunday is your last day of freedom. You spend the day feeling the tick of the clock. Despite all your hopes to "really live" over the weekend, it was a bit more mundane and anticlimactic. Then, on Monday, the countdown begins again, and your mind is off to the races.

Notice, in all your daily interactions a constant urge in yourself or others to interject, like you're listening but not hearing each other.

Sit in a coffee shop and listen. You will find many busy people plowing through conversations about trivialities—the minutiae of daily life. Everything's a crisis.

Again, we are simply not used to the type of interaction where one person listens without merely waiting for another chance to speak.

As a child, I remember being asked by a cousin to come over and play with the son of their Italian family friends, whom they'd met while living in Italy. He didn't speak a single word of English. I thought, *How can I play with this kid if we can't say anything?*

Interestingly, interactions with him were enhanced without words. The pressure was gone. We weren't burdened with thinking of things to say to avoid awkward pauses because there was *only* pause. Silence was expected and allowed, so there was no small talk; there was no "How do you like it here?" or "What do you do for fun?"

Instead, we became fully present in each moment. We were more perceptive of hand signals and expressions. There was still plenty of listening, just not for words. It was about enjoying the beingness of another person. There was a greater purity in doing something mundane like kicking a soccer ball back and forth. It was easier to concentrate and be present.

Conversely, a few years ago, I remember chatting with a friend about something deeply personal, yet she seemed distracted. After a stream of "uh-huhs," I realized she wasn't listening to a word I was saying. She looked at me every so often and nodded, but it was a blank look. I *felt* it. Then, back to her phone, distracted and off someplace else, only chiming in with an opinion having nothing to do with the details of what I'd shared. Upon realizing this, I stopped midsentence and simply sat. She didn't notice.

More recently, I remember a conversation with a retired military leader. About an hour into it, I realized it wasn't a conversation at all since I hadn't said anything, nor did I have an opportunity. It was an hour of him on a soapbox. Based on his behavior, he perceived it as a pleasant interaction, but that's because he felt comfortable in his role—his familiar role as the center of an interaction, demonstrating of his value. But he didn't know what a normal two-way conversation was like because he was so accustomed to controlling the floor and giving opinions as others kowtowed to him. And he didn't have the slightest self-awareness about the amount of talking he was doing, as if there were nothing left for him to learn.

"Great chatting with you," he said.

It wasn't a connection between two people of equal value. I had plenty to say, but it was nearly impossible to get a word in edgewise without interrupting. Once I realized that wouldn't serve any real purpose since his goal was not to connect with *me*, I just let him do what he was going to do anyway: talk while I listened. I wasn't a person; I was a role, a means to an end.

Often we are lost in the noise that reduces us to roles and unaware that in order to have a real interaction, all that's required is *being there*—something so few people can seem to do.

Over the years I have observed one client after another reflect on how their lives (and goals) seemed to slip away as if without their permission, leaving them dumbfounded. They reflected on their relationships and sometimes expressed that there was something missing in their daily lives that they couldn't define, not realizing they spent life in their heads.

Most of them felt the stress, the busyness, as something overwhelming they couldn't control; it was happening *to* them, not because of them. But, as an outsider, each situation looked different—relative. After all, I know single moms with two jobs and four kids that seem to get more done than some retirees who swear they're too busy to go on a walk twice a week and are stressed to the max.

*If you want to get something done,*
*give it to a busy person.*

**—ATTRIBUTED TO BENJAMIN FRANKLIN**

In other words, busyness is more often about the person than the situation, and few people can see that.

Where does your busyness come from? There are two types of busy. You can choose to be busy of your own accord, consciously, or it's reactive. It happens *to* you. You're always a moment behind. You aren't in *this* moment because you're busy reacting to the last. You're never quite here. The type of busyness discussed in this book relates to the more reactive busyness that defines the experience of many stressed, overwhelmed adults.

Eleven years ago, I was asked an ordinary question, but I never forgot it. I was working at a wellness center, and I experienced an interaction with a customer. It was common practice for me to greet guests, but this experience was different.

An older man entered the front door, smiling, and walked through the lobby before suddenly stopping in front of me. He looked at me and said something profound.

"How are you?" he asked.

It's not the words that were profound, but the presence in those words. He was *there*. He meant it, and I could feel that. He said something that almost everyone says, but the way he said it was different. He asked me a real question, and he wanted a real answer. He stood there and waited for it. I probably looked confused. Again, people are simply not used to that type of interaction.

I responded, and the result was a delightful yet brief conversation, and I remember it fifteen years later. Afterward, the man continued with his day and life, probably forgetting about the conversation moments later. It reminded me how rare such genuine interactions are and how a genuine experience can indeed be had in ordinary moments.

People crave authenticity because they're starved of it. And I never knew his name.

*People will forget what you said, people will forget what you did, but people will never forget how you made them feel.*

**—ATTRIBUTED TO MAYA ANGELOU**

"How are you?" *"Good, how are you?"* The words quickly roll off your tongue. You didn't really answer, and you're not asking, either.

"How are you?" *"Not too bad."* So you're bad, just not *too* bad. Fantastic.

"How are you?" *"Well, halfway through the week!"*

"How are you?" *"Hanging in there."*

"How are you?" *"I haven't had my coffee yet."*

"How are you?" *"It's Monday."* What would make you say that as if it's a good thing? Instead, say, "It's Monday!" You ought to look forward to Monday as any other day of the week. Monday should not have such a black cloud over it. Remember, there's no "work life" or "personal life"; there's just life.

"How was your weekend?" *"Too short."* It always is. Is there another answer?

We say things like that all the time—empty fluff language. If you've been in the corporate world, you know what I mean. How do people sign their emails in the corporate world? "Regards," or "Tx" ("Thanks"), or "Warmly," another fluff word. I've even seen corporate managers send emails of pure criticism, signed "Warmly." Is that supposed to mean something?

Or, better yet, they sprinkle "V/R" ("Very respectfully") into an email signature, as if one couldn't muster enough energy to write it without abbreviating. People can feel that. They can feel being reduced to roles, functions, means to ends.

You don't see them as a person in that moment, and you can't see the human on the other end because you've taken that humanity. You've reduced them—"respectfully," of course. But you don't mean that, either.

Certainly, I may offer a "Thank you." But I'm present with those words, even if they're written, and I *intend* to use them. Or I may simply sign my name. No fluff required.

Imagine if we spoke that way. Try it after your next work meeting. "*V* slash *r*, guys . . ." Or next time you hang up the phone, end the conversation with "Regards." If you wouldn't speak that way, why would you write that way?

If you aren't building people up, you're breaking them down.

Of course, there is often not enough awareness for there to be ill intent; the intent may be "professionalism," but the result will always be transactional. Humanity is left out of it.

This type of sterile atmosphere is prevalent in highly structured environments, corporations, and in the military.

With empty statements often a topic of discussion, I began occasionally signing emails to my colleague "Very disrespectfully, Ryan." And an equal response from her: "Coldly, Liz."

*Someone told me signing my emails with
"Best" is passive-aggressive, so I'm changing it to
"See you in hell" to eliminate any confusion.*

**—ANGELA MARIE**

We are conditioned to believe that our work is who we are. When it doesn't complete us, and it won't, we are left purposeless. Maybe you want to be a nurse, to "help people." If you're a cashier, are you less purposeful? Or are you just less? If you're defined by a role that doesn't complete you, who are you? You're "hanging in there."

People don't leave bad jobs; they leave bad situations created by bad leaders. They leave toxic cultures. Often, workplace culture is determined by a group of individuals (managers) promoted into roles based upon their past performance (or politics), not necessarily because they're the best fit for leadership.

The Peter Principle, developed by Laurence Peter, is the concept that most managers rise to the point of their respective incompetence. And they often, with the slightest authority and without proper knowledge of how to get the very best from people, drive workers away with their micromanaging. A micromanager is a lousy manager. Lacking self-awareness, a defining characteristic, they frequently blame staff for any discord. They fail to realize that leadership and management are two different things. Often, they see tasks to be managed, and roles, not people. And this was a source of unhappiness for so many of my clients who felt stuck at jobs they hated, helpless.

All interactions—as a friend, parent, brother, neighbor, coworker, or manager—soon become transactions, with all the dramas, miscommunications, and sterility, as soon as people stop being present and reduce each other to roles. What's missing is self-awareness, and few will achieve it.

We don't respond to a loved one; we react to them. We don't respond to an email; we react to it. We don't respond to a waiter; we react to him.

"How are you?" *"Good, how are you?"* you say quickly, without a thought.

But you aren't "good," are you? Apparently, you're bad, just not *too* bad.

Again, it's not that we have bad intentions. It's that we don't care, per se. We don't have time. We are in a rush, living that to-do list.

"Good" is not a real answer. Imagine the reaction you'd get if you answered honestly—some strange looks and raised eyebrows.

"Today, I'm not feeling well. I think I have a cold. Plus, my car wouldn't start this morning. I'm worried it will be expensive to fix. I had to get a ride to work. I don't want to be here today," you might say if you're honest.

"Well, I'm sorry to hear that," the other person might say. *And I'm sorry I asked,* they might think. Again, it wasn't a real question.

Let's assume you're more of a glass-is-half-full type of person.

"How are you?"

"I'm a bit tired on this rainy day, but I'll make the most of it. I'm excited to welcome our new coworker today."

"Great."

The moment it was asked, they were on to the next thought in a long stream of internal dialogue.

The feeling of busyness—the uncomfortable feeling of being overextended, rushed, and thus transactional—manifests as feelings of stress in the pit of your stomach. It's there no matter your socioeconomic class, age, or how busy you actually are.

"But I do have a lot to do!" some might say. And this is true because it's true to you. Yes, there are things you have to do, but it's mostly fluff—the tasks you bring on yourself, sign up for, or do with little to gain. Most often, decisions brought you to that place. And decisions can bring you out. "What decisions?" is a good question, and this book aims to explore that with you.

At times, I may be busy, even on a day off, because I make choices. I may exercise, visit someone, work on a project, and then go to a restaurant. But that's not the busyness most people experience in their discomfort of daily urgency. Busyness is the pressure looming in the background as they "make it through."

We make it through the kids' soccer games, or to the next paycheck, or to the weekend. Each day becomes the management of daily tasks, dishes, laundry. It's not long before the busyness becomes a weight that's too heavy to lift, and it soon grows into learned helplessness. By a certain age, it's ingrained. We don't know any different. There's no frame of reference for what life could be like because we can't see how we keep ourselves stuck . . . until an event or trauma awakens us.

*The price of anything is the amount of life
you exchange for it.*

**—HENRY DAVID THOREAU**

Seconds before my first cardiac arrest at the young age of thirty, I knew it was happening. I knew I'd only seconds left. My field of vision narrowed, darkness on the fringes, like a tunnel becoming smaller and smaller. The darkness closed in, and my heart stopped.

Indeed, certain truths about your busyness will become clear in the end.

In the ICU, I lay connected to an assortment of wires and tubes. I became entranced by the monitor, by each wave of my heart's rhythm. It became my obsession: each line, each sound, and each terrifying instant a beat was late—a frightening reminder of my mortality as I walked the tightrope. I feel my pacemaker kick in even as I write this, along with another wave of dizziness . . .

But, lying there, I didn't think for an instant about work. And I surely didn't think about the to-do list. It never crossed my mind.

Before my second cardiac arrest, I uttered what I thought were possibly my last words: "Oh shit!" I could feel it coming, too, before the darkness. Then it was quiet.

I left the safety of the hospital with all the trepidation of a new swimmer pushing away from the wall for the first time. Soon thereafter and against my doctor's orders, I began driving and returned to work, connected to a myriad of wires that led to a portable heart monitor. I sat at my desk next to my blood pressure cuff—one at work and one at home. When the light blinks on my heart device beneath my desk, it downloads the information within my chest and sends it to the doctor. I'm still amazed.

Upon resuming sessions, I remember a client going on about why she didn't follow through with anything she said she'd do. She was "too busy," of course. And that may be true, but no client who's ready for change says this. When you're ready, you'll know. Otherwise, each reason is as valid as someone chooses it to be. Maybe it's the bathroom remodel. Or a car in the shop. If not one thing, it's another. Yet, perplexingly, I had clients with far more to do, like go to a job (which she did not), who seemed to get more done in three hours than this woman did in an entire day. Again, we can't see ourselves.

Busyness looked different to me. I became fatigued by all her ramblings. I was sick and not long out of the hospital (and surgery). I started to think about some life experiences from a different perspective. My problems, time, energy all seemed so clear to me, as if I were somehow separate from the humdrum in which my clients were lost. I seemed to be observing it from someplace else.

Each day a regurgitation of the same noise in her head, she seemed to repeat herself over and over again without knowing it. The goal, then, was to pull her into exploring that. *How can someone be happy carrying around all that?* I thought, clutching the lump in my chest, as I frequently do.

The curse of knowledge is that once you know something, you can't imagine not knowing it. It's the "red pill" in *The Matrix*.

I've walked the tightrope along the edge of darkness many times since then. When the paramedics came for me at work, as I teetered on the fringes of consciousness, again, slumped over in sweat, I remember the fear—the fear of the darkness and the lonely desperation for comfort as I held on for as long as I could. A kind voice meant everything.

My colleague Liz was great. She was one of those who asked, "How are you?" and meant it. I felt that. She asked that question many times, but she always wanted a real answer. No matter what we chatted about, she was always *there*. And you never know the impact one moment like that can have—the small kindnesses. And, again, you can never tell what someone is going through, and they're always going through something.

*Today you could be standing next to someone who is trying their best not to fall apart. So whatever you do today, do it with kindness in your heart.*

**—AUTHOR UNKNOWN**

So the next time someone asks you how you are, say, "I'm excellent, as always." *Choose* that. Choose how you're going to show up in the world. Then, ask them too, but mean it, because one day the noise will be silent, and things will look different.

# CHAPTER THREE

# Becoming You:

## *Your Relationship with Yourself*

*The need for acceptance will
make you invisible in this world.*

**—JIM CARREY**

**Lessons from Near Death:**

*The person you create yourself to be in all that you do so you can matter is not really you. You can't become who you already are. You'll miss that person in the end.*

## IDENTITY CRISIS

You are not your resume.

Nor am I. I am not a writer; I am a person who writes. Of course, you can't have a relationship *with* yourself; you *are* yourself. But this chapter is an exploration of the environment in your head that creates "you."

So, who are you? Ask your ex-partner after a bad breakup, your mother, and your coworker, and you'll get some vastly different responses. Two people will always have a different experience of the same thing. Which is true? Both and neither.

I remember once listening to the most beautiful music I could imagine and was always perplexed how anyone could dislike it. We might all have ears but hear something very different. The same is true in every area of your life.

Whether you're a billionaire, celebrity, clerk, homeless person, or are in prison, everyone wants to be seen as who they really are: someone who matters. They want to be seen as more than their money, more than their situation, or more than their mistakes.

But defining that person can be difficult.

What one person can't see about himself is what everyone else sees. The discrepancy between how we think others see us and how we want to be seen can cause a lot of pain. This is because for many, their value comes from outside them. They don't realize their worth isn't something that has to be earned. Instead, they look for it through comparisons; that's where meaning comes from. No one is rich unless someone is poor. No one is popular unless someone isn't.

In other words, we look to other people to tell us our value, but we are looking in the wrong places. This chapter explores that—the realization that most people spend much of their lives chasing visions of themselves that have nothing to do with who they really are.

As a child, I remember suffering from crushing anxiety, my mind racing with endless thoughts and internal dialogue. I worried compulsively about anything and everything. Extremely introverted, I was quiet and had a natural drive to please or help people even when they didn't seem to deserve it.

Without realizing it, how I saw other people react to me only confirmed the reasons I was quiet to begin with—feelings I simply wasn't enough. I believed those feelings, and my behaviors supported those beliefs.

Without conscious awareness of how I was keeping myself stuck in my own mindset and unable to break free, my life was driven by the need to constantly fit in, find my place, and find my identity. Identity is where we think our worth comes from, and we do everything in our power to build it. We change our clothes, shoes, friends, cars, activities, and anything we can to bring us closer to how we want to be seen—to manipulate others' perceptions of us so we can feel better about ourselves. We can't see that nothing we can ever do will truly control how others see us.

People don't need validation to be worth something. The drive to "fit in" can last a lifetime. Even people who state that they "don't care" about fitting in will see how much they've learned to need it. But in the end, you'll realize how much of that time was wasted in suffering when it didn't need to be.

You're already all you'll ever be. And you don't fully know who that is. How could you?

To know themselves, most people constantly reevaluate their place in life through comparison in an unending battle to bolster their own worth and avoid threats to that worth. They are superior or inferior, better or worse.

If a close friend strives to "make it big" as an actor or rock star or author, for example, part of you, even unconsciously, wants them to fail. You *want* the drama. You want drama so long as you're not a party to it. If you don't believe this to be true, answer this: what, specifically, is entertaining about the many reality shows that are so popular?

Of course, you *want* to support your friend if they become famous, but you wish it was you. It's why "friends" and long-lost relatives come out of the woodwork when someone becomes famous; they want a piece of it. Their success makes you feel worse about yours, or lack thereof, and that triggers pain in you. It should've been *you* that got the record deal and not your friend because you're a better musician. You deserve it more. You worked harder. *You* should be the one with *that* house, or car, or job, or spouse. So there's resentment. There's pain in the constant reminder that their arrival proves *you* did not arrive. It's "unfair."

It's different if you don't know them; they don't threaten your sense of worth. So the drama is a distraction. You can lose yourself watching that drama unfold on television. They're not people, but caricatures—also roles. We watch as they live lavishly, consumed by social dramas that define their daily experiences. If there's nothing else to buy—if you can afford everything—then all that's left is status. We can live vicariously through them by immersing ourselves in their opulence but without all the drama associated with *being* them. They become spectacles.

We're excited that Aiden is cheating on his wife and that she's about to find out in this episode because it's shocking. What will her reaction be? Never mind her pain as a real person; we don't know her. Her pain becomes others' strange pleasure. Nothing attracts a crowd quicker than a good fight. The excitement reminds you you're alive, and that's intoxicating, so long as you aren't involved and are free of the pain.

There's more pain in seeing people you know get ahead because of the familiarity. The more shared history you have with someone, the more perceived limitations you place upon them. Thus, any break from that perception in terms of their success almost feels phony.

Your friend Johnny wrote a book. He's "just Johnny," so what makes *him* qualified? Never mind how qualified he *actually* is; it's almost always going to seem "presumptuous" because he's "ordinary."

Amanda, the neighbor who babysits your kids, just got a record deal. She's *someone* now. Will she still talk to you, or will it go to her head? Or if you think she stinks and doesn't deserve it, will it go to yours?

Perception begins to change the moment other people react differently to a person.

Value gaps are perceived deficits you feel in different situations through comparison. Most people don't know they're doing this, since comparison manifests as feelings. But they will always try to bridge those gaps to feel better about themselves. Comparison (or separating from others) is fine so long as *they* are the winner of that comparison.

Many people work very hard to convince others that they "don't care what people think" about them. They are "unapologetically themselves." But they also care that others know that. Often, they profess that they "don't care" as a defense mechanism driven by the fact that they actually do care, very much. They're vulnerable, and professing that they don't care is a way to build protective walls. If they didn't care about other people's opinions of them, they wouldn't expend the energy to profess something like that. Difference is painful if it's *too* different. We want uniqueness, not ostracism. Ostracism is like death.

Growing up, a group of kids were perceived as outcasts. That is to say, they were awkward and didn't fit into mainstream social groups. They kept to themselves and wore black trench coats and other gothic attire—a "nonconformist" trend for kids who didn't fit. I realized their general desire was to buck the popular, preppy trends of the masses as they sought identities in places they felt accepted.

But in all their nonconforming, what did they do? They conformed to other nonconformers—nonconformist conformists, loneliness masquerading as empowerment. A true nonconformist doesn't care if everyone does something or no one does. They do something because they want to. Not conforming simply doesn't cross their mind because they're not trying to create separation. But most nonconformists care very, very much and seek to belong under the guise of not needing it.

If you like a shirt, wear it. Everyone may wear it, or no one may wear it. If people like it, great. If people don't like it, great. It's a shirt that you like, and that's the end of it.

Imagine Brent, a popular young man at a local gym. He walks, dresses, and speaks a certain way to paint the picture of his identity— someone important and trendy, someone who belongs. Upon seeing a friend in the locker room, Brent gives him a trendy handshake or hug. They converse mostly about their social lives and what they're doing for the weekend (hint: it's a party).

Like many people, Brent curses needlessly as conversation filler because he thinks it dictates perception; he demonstrates his position and becomes "more" in his own eyes. It soon becomes a habit he doesn't realize. It's a way of speaking born from the way Brent sees himself; it's posturing.

Listen to such a conversation in a men's locker room. Brent may change his tone, words, and behaviors depending upon a situation, much as a chameleon changes his colors. He sounds different in a locker room than when speaking to the old lady down the street. It's posturing as an attempt to force perception in ways that match how Brent sees himself.

Many people work very hard to appear a certain way, especially as they vehemently deny it. Soon, such behaviors become ingrained habits as they become increasingly unaware they're doing it.

Think of the mind as a label maker. It quickly pigeonholes every person, place, or thing according to how each compares in value. To do this, you've got to make quick judgments about people to categorize clearly. This doesn't make the label true, but it does make it true to you.

People are shoveled into categories—Democrat or Republican, pro-life or pro-choice, man or woman, right or wrong, good looking or not, popular or not, high value or not. As people become hardwired to see what "value" is and how it's earned, they lose the ability to see things as they actually are—until they're temporarily snapped out of the trance by a life-altering event. Then they realize they've spent their entire lives giving attention to the wrong things.

Most of what they thought was true about themselves and their lives was actually just a perception, assumption, or opinion crafted by the label maker. There is great confusion over what is real about a person because, in part, most information is framed to fit each identity, and the individual doesn't look for evidence beyond that.

In other words, it's impossible to discern fact from fiction if someone isn't open to finding what's true (or not) about a person or situation. Discernment requires an open mind that's not married to a certain point of view. That's not most people. Most people hear something and assume it's correct, especially if what they hear aligns with their beliefs, and especially as media technology tailors information to a person's preferences.

Why can't they be open minded? Because of their identity. If they're open minded, they also open themselves to being wrong, which makes them vulnerable. If they're wrong about one thing, what else are they wrong about? And the house that Jack built crumbles to the ground. Being wrong does not allow people to feel secure in their identity, and how they feel means everything. So their opinions are like gospel.

The more close-minded someone is, the more value they derive from their identity and the more threatened they are by losing it. Opinions can't be shaky, or there's doubt about what's real. Ambiguity is like poison. They may even choose to believe something no matter what information comes to light because this vulnerability is terrifying. To always be right and secure, they must completely identify with a side—a side provides them a definition of themselves, as if to say, "That's me."

*It is the mark of an educated person to search for the same kind of clarity in each topic to the extent that the nature of the matter accepts it.*

**—ARISTOTLE**

It's the mark of an educated mind to entertain an idea without necessarily accepting it.

I recently stopped at a light behind a vehicle with a "Democrat and Proud" bumper sticker. This sticker could have been any political or religious affiliation. "Got Jesus?" said another. Is there anything less sacred than reducing a prophet to a bumper sticker inspired by an old milk ad? It's not enough that someone has beliefs; they must profess them to others as if to say, "Yes, I belong to *this* group, and *this* is who I am." But it's limiting. You shovel yourself into a category without openness to anything outside of it.

With the professing of such belief, you take on that identity and experience a relatedness that only occurs with its announcement. That's a key to identity—the announcement that it's yours.

So, who are you?

You're "pro-choice" and are thus shoveled into a category. The opposing side can then properly oppose you; "pro-choice" must mean you're "pro-abortion." But just because someone is "pro-choice" doesn't mean they're pro-killing babies. Perhaps there is more nuance to their viewpoints, but no one bothers to ask those questions or start a dialogue because they've already made that person into opposition— into a category. *They* are defined, and "the others" are defined.

It's not just marriage, but "gay marriage." No one talks about their "straight marriage."

If you're a Republican, congratulations, you've inherited all the views that come with that, and without deviation. If you're a Democrat, congratulations, you've inherited all the views that come with that, and without deviation. One category or the other. What do they call someone with views that are all over the place? What do they call people who reserve the right to change their minds as they collect information? Nothing. They don't belong to anything, and that's their reward.

You're either for big government or small government, not simply just enough government to take care of what's needed when it's needed. It's either always too big and therefore treads on you, or always too small and drives a wedge between the haves and have-nots. You belong to this party or that party. There's not much room in between, especially if you want to get elected.

But just because someone votes for a political candidate doesn't mean they approve of everything they do or even like them. Again, might there be more nuance to their opinion before they're shoveled into a category?

It's simply easier to understand opinions in black-and-white terms— to make arguments binary, right and wrong. That's how identity works; there's you and those like you, and the others.

Who are you?

"I'm a Christian," you might say. Oh, are you? Perhaps it just wasn't convenient at the club the night before or when you had to deal with your ex. Your behavior wasn't quite "Christian," but you can't see that.

I recently saw a young man wearing a "WWJD" (What Would Jesus Do?) bracelet as he rapped along to gangster rap, with the expletives flowing like wine. Jesus would rap, apparently.

What many people mean when they call themselves "Christian" is that they believe in God, whatever that means, although they don't practice Christianity's teachings full time. The rest is the comfort of the label—that it's enough to believe what they believe and that however many missteps occur whenever they're out doing whatever they want, it's all good because they'll always be forgiven, God still loves them, and so forth and so on. They belong to that religion, after all.

Thus, their "Christian-ness" is more about how they feel about themselves under the label "Christian" than who they actually are or how they behave, which they can't see. In other words, their Christianity resides in their belonging to a group that believes and in the tenet that because you aren't part of that group, you inherently need saving from your own evilness and damnation. This is the "club Christian."

Your neighbor can't figure out her smart TV, but apparently she knows how all of existence works. Plus, it's in a book. Actually, how many people do you know who can *really* explain how a TV works? Or anything else they use on a daily basis? How many people can explain how their own body works?

In any religion, what makes us think we are entitled to an answer to life's questions or that we are even capable of understanding those answers? We try by reducing questions of existence into something understandable. But what if you said, "I don't know," and let it be okay? A truth seeker will be open to all possibilities, including the absence of an answer. They are curious with a reserved right to change their mind.

So, who are you?

"I'm an activist!" Sure, there are people who are extremely passionate about an issue. But a portion of those people have also created themselves as moralists. In doing so, they shape their perceptions of themselves as people who, in their righteousness, are more moral than you.

Be the change. Discuss the change, not the label.

So, who are you?

"I'm American!" a patriot says with great enthusiasm.

Think America is the greatest country ever? That's precisely the notion that would make it *not* the greatest—the arrogance in thinking that we are. And that arrogance is bipartisan.

Is it the greatest because we're here? Makes sense. Perhaps it's the freedom. But isn't the United Kingdom free? Canada? France? Germany? Italy? Australia? Sweden? We can be grateful for many things, yes, but that doesn't make us *better.* Nor does the irony that we were founded on the notion of freedom yet promptly worked to exterminate one race and then enslaved another. Freedom isn't free.

Does expensive healthcare make us the greatest? The leadership? Certainly not the humility. Nor is it true independence; so few products are actually made here. We are part of a larger whole but can't quite see it.

What is freedom, exactly? It's an idea. What we really have is an *allotted degree* of freedom (which isn't exactly freedom), or else we'd have no governance. Our elections are a staple of this "freedom." That is, popular "votes" have no real authority in determining the outcomes of elections; we have delegates for that. But we do offer suggestions.

Americans sing about this "land of the free and home of the brave" that was free only to some. And how can you possibly generalize bravery, a character trait, as characteristic of absolutely everyone just because they live here? Is that to say that another country isn't brave too? What country thinks they're not brave? What does it mean if every country sings of its bravery, believing that quality unique to *that* country? You always have to look for character at the individual level; otherwise, it's just belongingness—part of a label.

Your country is the greatest because it's yours. It's part of your identity. This is not to say that you, or we, are not the greatest. This is to say that *there is no greatest.* The "greatest" is an idea about how we compare, and you can see how we fare. By comparison, America consumes a lot, loves guns, and is number one in defense spending—not literacy, employment rate, or any other category.

We must stop thinking like everything's a ranking. We are all just people; that's it. There are no good or bad countries. There are only people, their beliefs, and their decisions.

Today, I turned on the news, and a newscaster was engaged in a fiery rant about how recent polls had indicated that national pride had dipped a bit. Then she said, "America is the greatest country on earth, period." Imagine how that comes across; imagine watching a foreign newscaster say that of their country. It's off-putting. Imagine an individual saying that to you about themselves. Part of what makes a person great is their humility and that they don't know of their greatness.

Imagine encountering a Chinese person who is very vocal about their country being the best. How do you think many Americans would respond? Imagine a new superhero—"Captain China," or "Captain North Korea"—who fights the evil empire of [insert enemy here, which is America in this case]. Is that self-aggrandizing?

When North Korean soldiers march in some outlandish tribute parade, Americans tend to chuckle and wonder how any society can be so brainwashed. Or we look at North Koreans pledging allegiance to their "Dear Leader" as further evidence of such brainwashing. I mean, how could anyone be so brainwashed? Imagine a society raising their children to recite a pledge, in unison, every single day as they "pledge allegiance to the flag" of the greatest country in the history of the universe (and God's favorite). Good thing that's not *us*. God shed his grace on thee, and only thee.

Are your rights "God-given?" In other words, God actually gave you those rights? Personally?

The Constitution is seen as almost divine, created by a surely well-intended group of men, but only certain men, who bestowed freedoms defined by them only to a group of men determined by them, and we've decided that at no other time in history did God create such a great group of guys. We're a staunch defender of the Constitution and take each word as God's . . . unless it doesn't support our views. Then, we've got some wiggle room.

"American first!" a political candidate shouts from a podium. Both candidates conveniently have perfectly opposing views with no overlap. And, according to them, just so you know, if you support a candidate's opposition, there will be a zombie apocalypse.

Of course, every country's leaders care about their country's "interests," even at the expense of someone else. "From now on, Russia first!" a candidate (the only candidate, ever) says during a Russian election. How does that sound to a non-Russian?

If each country were a person, you'd find most of them reprehensible. In no way would we find the characteristics and attributes that define countries' associations acceptable if those characteristics and attributes were found in individual people. People behave in groups in ways they wouldn't, generally, as individuals. Again, it's the belongingness.

*Many a man's reputation would not know his character if they met on the street.*

**—ELBERT HUBBARD**

Every company and military in the world has "values." Loyalty, service before self, and so on, all the same values said in different ways. What does it mean to truly embody those values? Just saying that you do? No one would say otherwise.

We explain to our children the qualities of a good person—humility, for example. We talk about selflessness. We talk about tolerance. While there are a select few people that actually emulate such qualities, again, those qualities are usually out the window when people are in groups. They *become* the group.

"I'm New York strong" or "Virginia Beach strong" or "America strong," you might say after something bad happens—a pandemic or mass shooting. What does that mean, exactly? Nothing; it provides an emotional boost—a coping. What makes that city's "strong" so much stronger or different than another? It feels different because it's *your* city. Would a mayor say otherwise? Would anyone? "Strong, brave, and courageous" describes any group to which you belong. You live where all the strong people live. "We're in this together!" And what does *that* mean? No one knows. But it does garner reactions.

Your country, your skin color, your hair color, your political party, your religion, your relationships—*that's* you. Are you not more nuanced than that? Where does your value go if those things disappear?

You can be grateful for your life, yes, but thinking that those things for which you're grateful make you better is arrogance. A better situation, better clothes, better shoes, better appearance, better bank account, better talent, better grades—none of that makes anyone better.

History has shown how "winners" become humbled. There was a time, perhaps until the Vietnam War shifted perception, that Americans thought they couldn't lose. Winners can't lose; pride makes losing almost impossible to believe. Every decision was right because we made it. It was the "good guys" versus the "bad guys," and, in our stories, the good guys always come out on top. It was difficult, even threatening, for many people to digest the idea that their country wasn't infallible. Infallibility was inherent in their identities.

This mentality is not unique to one country or leader or time period. It exists in people who can't see beyond themselves, in their bubbles, and don't realize it.

In World War II, Americans dropped two atomic bombs. Evacuated Japanese children returned to rubble to find the charred remains of their parents. Beyond enemies or allies, and right or wrong, there are people; there's humanity.

Even in winning, there are no winners.

# CHAPTER FOUR

# Never Enough:

## *Validation, Money, and Stuff*

*At some point, when you create yourself to make it, you're going to have to either let that creation go and take a chance on being loved or hated for who you really are, or you're going to have to kill who you really are and fall into your grave grasping on to a character that you never were.*

**—JIM CARREY**

### Lessons from Near Death:

*Seek experiences as an explorer of your life, not for what they get you. Never confuse learning or achieving something for its own sake with learning or achieving something for how it makes you look because the only person that really cares is you, and you've wasted your time for nothing.*

## CHASING SUCCESS

"What do you want to be when you grow up?" we are often asked when we are young. Even then, you're not a person but rather a role to become. We grow up believing we have to become a role to *be* someone, but those beliefs are peppered by all the years of conditioning by others about what you should and shouldn't do and what is and isn't possible. Everyone seems to know what's best for you. And don't worry, they'll let you know.

"You can be anything you set your mind to as long as you don't give up," says a mother to her young daughter.

"Mom, was it always your dream to be a waitress?"

As kids, we dream of being fighter pilots or firefighters, musicians, doctors, or world travelers. Kids see possibilities. Adults see risks.

This is not to say that you can do anything you put your mind to, like many parents or public service announcements profess with hollow words. For example, I'm not sure my dream of playing in the NFL is going to work out, no matter what I "set my mind to."

The issue with dreams is that they're often tied to an outcome to be had or an achievement of some sort that will make you into someone more than you are. You're not *this* person until you've achieved *this*. And so, growing up, anything short of its achievement is failure. Many people dream of becoming famous. No one dreams of becoming a salesman at an electronics store.

You have control over your behaviors, yes, but never outcomes.

At a young age, we set our sights on this better version of ourselves and call it a "dream."

"I want to be a famous actor," you say when you're young.

"You'd better have something to fall back on," your parents may say after you enthusiastically share your big, new goal.

"Just make sure it offers health insurance" is wise advice, but it isn't quite the initial reaction you'd hoped for; it's a bit more tempered than the reactions you were getting when young and the world was still your oyster.

That first reaction, one of fear and skepticism, takes the wind from your sails. It's all you can do to muster the courage to keep going as you walk the motivational tightrope. They're happy to tell you what *they* would do (which is never what you're doing).

Then there's talk about backup plans and retirement savings. It's because they love you, and they worry. And so the dream changes to "stability." What once made you a dreamer is traded for what seems safe. It's not that stability isn't wise, but it's often an excuse to stay within the well-defined boundaries of your comfort zone.

It's not that being an actor is a bad thing. Or being a rock star. Or a model. Or a professional athlete. But that's not the draw. The draw is the caricature—how we *see* famous actors. Who wants to be a great actor if they're not famous? Ask a child that same question. Being an actor isn't big enough; you've got to be known.

Your family, teachers, and everyone you know mean well, of course, but the more shared history you have with someone, the less likely they will see you outside of a box, your situation and role, and that's limiting. You tend to be pigeonholed because of this familiarity.

This is when initial seeds of self-limiting beliefs are planted in your mind. You can see how others view you, and that greatly influences your identity.

You're "just Matt," according to your brother. He doesn't see you as a renowned and respected military general, business executive, actor, or astronaut. To him, you're always "just Matt." Often, this discrepancy between how someone wants to be perceived and how they think they are perceived drives kids to rebel. They may act in all sorts of ways to create themselves into someone that makes them feel whole.

Your siblings, parents, and friends (or anyone with a long shared history) also see you in this familiar way, in a box. If you don't believe this is true, imagine a sibling who achieves a prestigious title. Who are they to you? The same person they were before.

Consider Johnny. Johnny grew up an awkward kid, ate glue in school, was chubby, and had a passion for video games. To his family, he's "just

Johnny." They don't see him as a prominent cardiologist, which is his role today. Nor do they tap into his vast medical expertise as fully as they could—again, because he's "just Johnny." No matter how successful he becomes, he will always be "Johnny"—the same kid who once ate glue.

*If you think you are enlightened,*
*go spend a week with your family.*

**—RAM DASS**

It will take Johnny's full presence not to live in the constant commentary of these self-limiting beliefs. He will have to understand that those beliefs are not him and that no other role is either. He is just a person who gets up each day and makes decisions that are either aligned with who he is or not. The rest is noise.

The moment Johnny lets people enter his mind, they'll never leave. To avoid letting them in, Johnny must accept others' opinions as just that—opinions—and understand they have nothing to do with who he is.

"What does your son do?" a man asks his new neighbor during a chat after checking the mail.

"He's an [actor, writer, musician, comedian, or some other 'risky' endeavor that doesn't meet expectations of what's a normal, safe, or familiar job]."

"Oh. Neat," he says, assuming all sorts of things about his neighbor's son without knowing him. The son is a "starving artist" or it's just a "hobby," and it doesn't fit conventional views of what a "regular job" should be. But if he eventually becomes famous, everyone "knew he would make it" all along.

You will always be seen as ordinary until you're not, or small until you're not. *Accept this.* There will always be doubt because you're familiar. You're common. But that's not true, either. You're neither a success nor a failure. You're a person, and your purpose here is to live your life. But until that time of clarity, you will live in a box of your own making.

So, who are you?

What's the first thing you ask when meeting someone for the first time?

"So, what do you do?"

Their resume is not who they are; that's their situation, a description of themselves as roles. Yet you instantly form opinions about this person without knowing it. Then, you can determine their value relative to yours, how you perceive your self-worth relative to them, and how they may affect your value through association.

"What do you do?"

"I'm the CEO of a Fortune 500 company."

Imagine the dynamic of that conversation.

"What do you do?"

"I'm a clerk."

Now imagine how the dynamic differs.

"I'm an Oscar winner."

"I'm homeless."

Like it or not, our bearings shift in each scenario to correspond to perceptions of value. You put that person in a box because you view them and the role—their current situation—interchangeably. Consider speaking to a four-star general. Do you communicate differently or feel any particular way that's different from talking to the man who pumps your gas? Yes, most people do.

Again, consider the example of the CEO and the clerk. You don't know that this clerk will one day become CEO of a large company. The person is the same, yet the role is different. If you knew this information about his future when you knew him as a clerk, would that affect your perception of him? Would you speak to him differently? What if you knew Bill Gates as a child with knowledge of his future? What if he somehow ended up in your high school science class? You'd probably pay a lot more attention to him. Some people would even attempt to become his best friend. Suddenly, knowing nothing about him as a person, you see his value differently.

Most people speak to each other based upon how they perceive value relative to their own. When you speak to someone of perceived higher value, you reflect that. When you speak to someone of perceived lower value, or importance, you reflect that. You don't necessarily treat them poorly, but you do treat them differently, even if unconsciously.

If you don't believe this to be true, ask yourself if there is anyone you could meet—a celebrity or military general or anyone else—that would make you nervous. Why are you nervous? Because they're someone of certain importance? But you don't know them. How do you know of their importance? Because you're told of their importance through their role—their fame, accolades, or accomplishments.

As I approached the end of my college term, I worked as a waiter at a local restaurant. "So, are you a student?" a customer once asked after I greeted them. I was, but the implication in their tone was that I must be a student because this type of job wasn't a good career—as if no one would possibly choose it if they had the choice.

Might the customer have assumed so because of my youth? Maybe, but my non-student coworkers had to endure much the same. Some of them, in fact, had worked there for many years. Some did so because it freed their days to be home with the kids. Some liked the job. They liked connecting with a diverse group of people—the social aspect. One was retired and thought it was a great way to get out of the house. And in the right situation, the cash was good.

We assume things about people, and then we box them in.

Every morning, I go to a drive-thru coffee shop. I know the worker at the window, an older woman who's been married for forty years—exceptionally friendly and always smiling. After getting to know her, I discovered that her income was secondary, a supplement to her husband's and not critical to her survival. Her job gave her the flexibility to raise her children while making extra money, and since she was a bit of a coffee enthusiast who enjoyed people, she continued working there. She liked it. Status never entered into it. She simply decided that she was going to love what was good about it. The cost of a different choice was too great.

*You* get to decide how you're going to show up in the world.

For most, they can't imagine living this way; they're mentally attached to what they think makes them valuable.

When a military general walks into a room, people stand. Do people stand for the person or the role? If everyone stands for the cashier, what happens to the perception of that role? What effect does it have on that person?

Many employers don't hire people; they hire roles. And if they focus purely on roles, roles are all they'll get. There will be no ownership of the experience, and employees will disappear when something better comes along. An employee's experience of an organization's culture will always reflect the degree to which it has reduced human beings to roles.

What's the cost of that role? Every role has a cost.


*What's living? Going to the office for fifty years?*

**—JIDDU KRISHNAMURTI**


## KEEPING UP WITH THE JONESES

Most of our lives, we work all day to afford the things we can't enjoy because we're too busy working all day to afford them. I have never looked at a fancy car with the best rims and thought in any particularly positive way about the driver—or any way at all. Instead, I wonder, *What was the cost, in time, for those rims?*

If you have money, great. It's a useful tool. So, what will you do with it? Is it helping you or adding to your mass—the sum total of what's necessary to maintain it? Again, what doesn't add takes away.

While these questions may not mean anything to a twenty-something who's living a life of endless tomorrows as they stand in line for the latest, greatest iPhone (that's virtually the same as the one they have), the cost in time will mean more later in their life. Keeping up with the Joneses is not worth that cost.

I remember a neighbor of mine many years ago who was single with no children and lived alone in his large home. He worked long hours and would regularly leave town for weeks at a time. It always perplexed me why he needed such a large home (in a poor market), despite never being there. Even a roommate would help mitigate that cost.

Perhaps it was an investment property—an unlikely scenario since he sold it less than two years later. But, again, there are ways to mitigate that cost that don't involve letting an empty house sit. You can only be in one room at a time. How many offices or guest rooms do you need?

Often, people make decisions based not on what makes sense but on the "natural next step." We attend school, purchase a car, purchase a home, get married, go on a honeymoon, and have children. We do all the things society expects of us. But just because you *can* do something doesn't mean you *should*.

Imagine a young woman drowning in student loans preparing for her wedding. Her parents spent twenty-five thousand dollars for a single day. "But it's for her special day," they might say. The money is for memories that most certainly can't be had without crystal stemware, a live band, or satin wedding invitations.

What's this wedding really about? What's important?

"It's what I want," a bride says as she continually adds to her registry. It's not enough that she's surrounded by those she loves, some of whom will spend thousands traveling long distances on her special day; they're asked to bring a gift from a very convenient list. After all, nothing says "I love you" like a grill cover or carbon monoxide detector (which are very useful). And if you're not kidding yourself and are a well-meaning human, gifts are required. Presence is not enough.

If you want to give a gift, give it. But if you're asked for it, then it's not a gift at all.

Then there's the honeymoon. Then the baby shower. It's what's expected.

What does an affluent couple do? The same. They ask for gifts. Maybe they ask for higher-value gifts. Or perhaps they could ask, in lieu of gifts, for a donation on their behalf to a local charity. Then again, they do need new bath mats . . .

"Tradition" can be the worst reason to do something, especially if it's a bad idea. But it's part of "who you are." You're the person who fits into that tradition, that neighborhood, that religion. That mold. You're the person who went to that school, makes that amount of money, or has that car. Who cares? *You* do, no matter how many times you say otherwise. Because that's "who you are."

Most people don't know who they are; they can't because they look outward. They chase visions of themselves with an insatiable appetite for things to define them. They want more—more titles, awards, degrees, accolades, money, and validation. They chase these shiny things, sometimes collecting them like trading cards. They think these things will make them more themselves, but they don't.

Sometimes, when people "make it big," they're surprised to find they're on an island. They've become someone, but it's not *them.* Deep down, something is still missing in their lives, but they can't quite put their finger on it. They may be on top of the world one day and, with a single misstep, hated the next.

Give a person money and fame, and observe what happens when you suddenly take it away. They will often quickly spiral out of control and suffer more than if they never had money or fame in the first place.

*A child that is not embraced by the village will burn
it down to feel its warmth.*

**—AFRICAN PROVERB**

They invented themselves to be important. Who are you inventing?

Imagine a former accountant has become "enlightened" after her yoga teacher certification. Although she has a degree in accounting, she also completed a part-time, eight-week training class down at the strip mall and has become a "holistic nutrition expert." As an expert, she is happy to show you the path to enlightenment, which involves essential oils. She perceives herself differently because she thinks that others do. She accomplished this by reinventing herself as a "spiritual person" who is *more* spiritual than you. Again, this is not to say that a person can't grow, change, or be spiritual. But ask the right questions. What are her motivations? Of course, there's only one answer she will provide without making herself vulnerable. And her motivations may be unconscious.

In this way, even education or training can be used to bolster someone's sense of worth. Look at a resume or social media profile; people call themselves all sorts of things. Your last role was "sales associate" at a mattress store, but now you're an "executive leadership coach." That's more aligned with how you see yourself, and it sounds better. What were you yesterday? What will you be tomorrow?

Sometimes, it's not about learning at all but about becoming—the gravitas that's realized with a string of letters after a name. How can you tell if it's posturing? One sign that someone is approaching their education for the wrong reasons is if they can't help but announce it when it makes no difference to a situation.

Sometimes those letters are the goal. Perhaps a young working professional aims to collect degrees as feathers in their cap, thinking that they're a step closer to a Nobel Prize with yet another random accolade, degree, or certification. That paper confirms their greatness. They paid too much, possibly to a for-profit institution (and, if they're not kidding themselves, they're *all* for profit), for the privilege of sitting at home on their computer as the grammar police check the assignment they just submitted—the quotes thrown together to appease the rubric and APA citation gods.

Congratulations. You now owe one hundred grand for the privilege of teaching yourself. Indeed, education has changed.

Some degrees, certifications, and licenses are critical to competence in a profession, so this is not to lump all of them together. But as education becomes big business, many are merely feathers in caps. The extent of this problem is uniquely American. Both schools and lenders use this knowledge to their advantage—both kids' naivete and peoples' drive for a very colorful feather. Schools don't merely offer loans; they market to and even prey upon people, sometimes with commission-driven telemarketing teams aptly called "advisors." These "advisors" pander to clueless kids who think it will rain opportunities (and money) when they graduate from Joe's Basement University accelerated (self-paced) online degree program that took six months to get. That'll be one hundred grand, please.

At the end of last year, the average university endowment was $1.4 billion, and it doesn't stop them from asking for more. And tuition goes up. Harvard's endowment last year was $53.2 billion. Even my local, small college has an endowment in the hundreds of millions. It *is* business.

Funding is super easy. Don't you want to "invest in yourself"? Your future? Don't you want "success"? *This* is the "natural next step," after all. Don't worry about the amount. It's what you're "supposed to do." Just fill out this form, and, like magic, your education is paid for. Worry about the fine print later.

Doing something because it's expected is dangerous. After all, how many kids have a clue what they want to do when they take that expensive step? And they don't know what they don't know. How many degreed, indebted baristas do coffee shops need? Again, there's nothing wrong with any particular profession. But no one goes to college (and incurs that amount of debt) specifically to make coffee. That's not what they thought they were getting at such an exorbitant cost. Otherwise, no one would do it. No one would carry that burden with such a low return.

How could they know? Kids have no concept of salaries or market trends. They don't know that tuition has increased disproportionately to income and educational quality (with less hands-on instruction). But their "advisors" gave them a "deal" for all that value. All they had to do was fill out a piece of paper to unlock their dreams, funded by a magical, selfless loan fairy.

The years tick by. Was it worth it?

This isn't to say learning isn't valuable. It is, always. But is there no other way to learn? If you want to learn, go learn. Where will you go? *Why* will you go?

Education ought to be about teachings, not titles. Not money. A good education teaches someone *how* to think not *what* to think.

## ATTACHED TO A TITLE

How can you tell if a military general is in the room (besides the symbols of their value that they literally wear on their chest)? Don't worry, they'll soon let you know, as will everyone else. How can you tell if a gas station clerk is in the room? You can't. But if that clerk wins the lottery, everyone knows.

A few months ago, I had a client with a doctorate. Upon meeting her, she said something peculiar to me: "For the purposes of this meeting, you can just call me Sandy." Worse are people who insist on being called "Doctor" in *every* situation: at the Christmas party, the kids' sporting events—*everywhere*.

"Great, thank you," I said. *How privileged I must be, given her importance.*

"Doctor" was written before her name all over everything she did. It was even reflected in her email address that began with "drsandy." Indeed, there are times when knowing someone is a doctor is useful. I want to know that my primary care physician is an actual doctor, for example. But, mostly, knowing someone has a doctorate in business or education is unnecessary when you're their lawn-care guy. And it doesn't just come up while chatting in the coffee line. In the context of my interaction, it was deliberately advertised to communicate her perceived value.

In other words, "Hi, I'm Sandy" would have sufficed.

"I've worked so hard to achieve that, and I deserve to be called 'Doctor,'" is a typical response when someone questions the overuse of a title or accolade. What are you gaining that you didn't have before you were called "Doctor"? What are you losing if you aren't called "Doctor"? And what, exactly, do you "deserve"? Do you mean your doctorate wasn't worth pursuing unless you can advertise it? Is it worth more since you can, regardless of the situation? Is it less real if people don't know you have it? Less true? What does announcing it do for you in your daily interactions or for the fact that you have it? What do you have? Why do you have it? Is that who you are?

Again, in many cases, it's not enough to have learned something. People must know you have a title, even in situations where it makes no difference. That's the surest sign someone derives their value outside themselves.

Consider the military, for example, where members are literally numerically ranked. Most people automatically and unconsciously rank others in terms of their perceived value, but this ranking is exacerbated if it's explicitly part of an organization's process. This conditions people to living in a way that plays to the worst of our nature, and in such a way that all but ensures they'll carry it with them for the rest of their lives.

In the military, E6s know if they're ranked first or ninetieth compared to other E6s. And E6s know they're ranked higher than E5s. This grade (or "rank") or perceived value difference, the carrot, exists no matter if you are a soldier, business executive, or even a politician, when someone has power (and status) over others.

Furthermore, officers are distinctly separate from enlisted military members. There is an inherent perceived value difference. Except in certain circumstances, they do not socialize. The nature of their association is a formal one, as the label "officer" has exalted the twenty-two-year-old know-nothing above the eighteen-year enlisted veteran. And, in some extreme cases, officers talk down to enlisted members almost as lower life-forms.

Or consider royalty—the idea that a person can be born into inherent superiority (and rule over others) because of their genes. It's tradition. It's identity. Their qualification to rule isn't based on ability or what's best for a country, but on the mere fact that they were born.

We are all equally as important or unimportant; those concepts are in the mind.

Some neighbors in a local retirement community find it extremely annoying that Bob signs his name "En emeritus," or "retired," and includes his credentials in absolutely every email correspondence. Bob was a university professor . . . over twenty years ago.

In this retirement community, there are former judges, police officers, executives, and others. No matter what the interaction, Bob makes it known, again and again, that he was someone special. "Dr. Robert Anderson, Professor Emeritus." *That's* who he is, and never forget it.

Living an entire life as a role, many retirees can't let go, sometimes experiencing aimlessness, so they cling to scraps of "who they are" before it disappears. Like Sandy, at what point is Bob just "Bob"? What difference does it make who he is when emailing his next-door neighbor about their new sprinkler system? In a retirement neighborhood, no one cares—except, apparently, Bob.

I once asked a client who she would be if she were no longer a soldier. There was a long pause.

"I really don't know," she said, nervous about her impending retirement.

Was she a soldier when she was born? No. Is she a soldier to her husband? No. I can't imagine her husband addressing her as "Sergeant." Will she be a soldier after retirement? No, although that doesn't stop soldiers from "living their rank" years after leaving the military. She is herself all the time; the rest is just circumstances. But "Diane" isn't satisfying. She is "Diane Johnson, SSGT US Army (retired)." What difference does it truly make? To her, a stay-at-home mom, a great deal.

"Did you know I have been waiting over thirty minutes for my meal!" an upset restaurant patron yelled at his server.

"I'm sorry, sir. I'll check on it right away," said the young man, who was clearly trying his best despite the restaurant's shortage of staff.

"I'm Major John Dawson, and I'd like to speak to your manager," the man said angrily, as if his rank made a difference to the situation.

Just imagine: "Oh, my deepest apologies, Major! I'll let the kitchen know you're a major; that way they can *really* try, instead of the lazy approach they take with regular people."

Who is Major Dawson? A person, actually, but don't ask him. And don't ask the military general I recently discovered who, with the taxpayer dollar, decided he wanted to celebrate . . . himself. There's nothing humbler than organizing a parade in your own honor.

Bob, Sandy, and Major Dawson identify with perceptions of themselves that a title allows—the validation of their importance.

"That's not me," you might say. "I treat (and view) everyone the same, and I don't think I'm better than anyone."

Oh? So, no part of you would perceive the gas station clerk and queen of England differently? Would you speak to them differently? If you met a person on the street and discovered they were a prince, would that change your behavior? For most people, it would, and they would have no awareness of it.

Of course, not all people are so attached to a title. I once had an enjoyable conversation with a man, only to find out later he had been a high-ranking military officer. I'd never guess it, and it never came up in our lengthy conversation. He was just "Paul." He was *there*—a person, without all the burdens of labels.

## SOCIAL LIFE

If people don't care to know you, they only care about what they get from you. This is sometimes a secret fear—that associations are little more than means to ends.

*The three predominant states of egoic relationships
are: wanting, thwarted wanting, and indifference.*

**—ECKHART TOLLE**

No, you don't have 1,647 "friends." But Facebook says you do. Often, you build value not only through association but through quantity—friends or followers. Each is tallied proof of your value. Do you not believe this is true? Imagine if you had only four friends, according to Facebook. How would you feel? It would sting, especially if others could see this number.

You met Johnny, friend number 235, while at a mutual friend's party seven years ago, and now you're "friends." You made small talk for about two minutes about nothing, and now he sees pictures of your family. Or, more realistically, you met someone who's a friend of a friend of a friend, and you'll never see them again. That is the case with most of your "friends." The nature of your friendship is a series of "likes." You can "like" his gym selfie, and he can "like" your hair—always a bathroom or car selfie.

Every Facebook "friend" can see every intimate detail you post. Yes, they can see that your kid is uniquely cute and intelligent, just like every other parent says of their own kid (without an ounce of bias).

"The doctors are saying he's supersmart. I mean, way more developed than other kids his age! He may be gifted!" a proud dad says as his son eats a crayon.

Sure, some people may genuinely care about news of your day-to-day life or your kids, but it's an infinitesimally small circle, like family. The vast majority of people, most of whom are little more than peripheral acquaintances, don't really care. Or they care, but peripherally; your news is just something to look at. The looky-loos, the nosy, just want to peer into your life to distract from their own—from all the anxieties and boredom of the mundane—and so are entertained. What are you distracting yourself from?

*Be careful who you open up to. Only a few people
actually care; the rest are just curious.*

**—ATTRIBUTED TO ERNEST HEMINGWAY**

Your profile becomes its own entity, separate from you but an extension of you and the person you've created. Your entire life is in your phone—emails, bank accounts, friends, medical information, pictures. It's your life in a box. The next generation of leaders will not know a life without them. For all the good that comes from such technology (such as the ability to find information at your fingertips about any topic), they will never experience life without the tether.

*When the phone was tied with a wire,
humans were free.*

**—AUTHOR UNKNOWN**

Use social media, but use it consciously, with intent, and connect with amazing people. It can be a fantastic tool. Share beautiful experiences and knowledge of this world, and communicate with those you love so they can appreciate it as you do. But don't *need* to use it. Don't make it your life.

Social media is not your diary. Not everything has to be documented for others to see. Is there not one moment that's just for you? Just because you didn't post it doesn't mean it didn't happen. Keep something for yourself. *Live it.*

Are you posting on social media to connect with people you care about, or are you posting for validation?

It's easy to "follow" someone on social media, such as a celebrity, and feel familiar with them, despite the fact that they don't know you exist. Your entire insight into their life is a carefully curated series of snapshots. But the perceived familiarity almost feels like friendship. Lost in the bolstered sense of worth through association, you can't see that you only know a perception of someone—a persona. Both the celebrity and the follower have a reciprocal, symbiotic association as they suckle the other's validation teat.

For celebrities, this following is a key driver of their fame. It's a business before it's an art.

"What kind of album did you make?" says an interviewer to a musician wearing sunglasses indoors. The musician once dressed in clothes from a local store, but now that society tells her of her increased worth through fame, she behaves accordingly.

She's the same as she was, which is enough, but don't tell her that. She went from wearing regular dresses to events to wearing something outlandish, like a flowerpot as a hat, because she sees herself (and wants to be seen) as a trendsetter to create further separation from others, increasing her value. She becomes a spectacle to stand out and drive reactions to her.

As long as it's called "art," it's genius. (Go to a Met gala.)

"Dancing, gettin' just a little naughty/Wanna get dirrty/It's about time for my arrival," said Christina Aguilera in her song "Dirrty." You know it's extra dirty because it's got the extra *r*, which means she's not messing around.

We can't help but complain about certain behaviors (that objectify or oversexualize a woman) but then perpetuate those behaviors through either engaging in them or happily watching them in others. We can't look away.

The pop star would never wear such attire in public when she was "a normal person," but now that she's a trendsetter, she can fully express herself. She's enjoyed the intoxicating euphoria of having "made it" as her fleeting followers constantly remind her.

"It's a concept album that tells my very personal story of love, breakups [many very dramatic end-of-the-world, twenty-year-old breakups], betrayal, and how I've grown as a woman," says the "artist" of her self-titled second album with the hit song "Yeah Yeah, Baby, Like That."

Did you know the song "WAP" is really about empowerment? Or about "embracing your sexuality"? It's okay because those artists are courageous in their self-expression. That's "so brave."

Anything goes as we become desensitized.

"How does this album differ from your first?" says the interviewer, who gushes over each and every word of a pop star as if their new song "Dat Ass" were going to change the world.

"It shows how much I've matured and how I can now express myself more fully because I have taken back control," whatever that means.

She's "made it."

But, deep down, she's afraid of losing that—afraid that none of it is real. Who would she be if she lost it all? It feels shaky, and people have short attention spans; they tend to forget when the next shiny new thing comes along. So she needs constant validation that she still matters and is relevant.

This is not to say there isn't talent there. But talent will always be obscured by the gimmicks. Until you take yourself seriously, no one else will. Let your work speak for itself. Make it about the music, not the persona.

Athletes, actors, and rock or pop stars are a kind of royalty that so many people aspire to. Men who throw a ball into a net or run another type of ball, in tights, into a painted area for points and get paid millions of dollars to play a *game* are royalty.

An actor attends yet another awards show as the world's most privileged gather. Some of those privileged don't miss the opportunity to enlighten their captive audience of their misguided ways. They then return to their mansions and sprawling estates, in some cases aboard private jets.

I recently watched a prominent actor accept an award. He accepted many awards that season, so rather than repeat the same speech for each award, he spoke of what he liked, specifically, about his other nominees. One by one, he explained how he admired each and how each was unique in their art. He was genuine, even becoming emotional about it. You could read the face of each of the other nominees as he spoke; he had lifted them up and offered insights into nuances of their performance lost on the lay public. Then, gracefully, he thanked them and walked away.

There were no political or personal ramblings. It was a masterclass in humility and gratitude and about the work itself. It wasn't self-aggrandizing. It was a rare light in a sometimes dark public discourse.

Value is all in the framing.

Does a seventy-five-year-old rock star marry a twenty-two-year-old supermodel if, instead of being a famous rock star, he's a local Walmart greeter?

"Do you want to go on a date?" says Bill, a pizza delivery guy, to an attractive young model.

"No."

"Do you want to go on a date?" says Bill, a Hollywood director, to an attractive young model.

"I'd love to," she says, her perception of him based on his power to "make her happy."

Why do you think there are exponentially more significant age gaps between many celebrities and their partners (the older partner being the celebrity) when compared proportionally to "ordinary" people? The young lady perceives the older celebrity a certain way before even meeting him, perhaps feeling she already knows him through his public persona. She sees his value (his power) every day because of others' reactions to him. The rock star, knowing this, will often be with the hottest person he can find. Because he can. And they both will use this association to bolster their careers, social media presences, and values—their identities.

Their children will encounter much the same illusion—that people know them because of their name. An actor's children may be talented, but they cannot escape the need to create their own identities and, in doing so, try to separate from their parents so they can believe their identities are real—that they're earned. But almost no celebrity's kid is an insurance salesman, accountant, or gas station clerk. *That's* not their identity. Their identity is wrapped up in the persona their name affords them. And as the famous sometimes realize, life can still be empty. It's why some of the most famous people on the planet are also the loneliest. It can be difficult to know what's real. It's a constant battle of understanding and reconciling you and the image of you.

What makes an identity real? Nothing you can do will make it more real. The need to make it real is in your head.

What we really want is a legacy. We are driven to make ourselves into people who will live forever through our legacies so that we can matter. But in trying to create that, we've made it self-serving.

In other words, a legacy isn't something you can create. If you need to create it, it's not a legacy.

The appeal of fame is in the idea that importance never dies. But it does. Your fame vanishes with you. What matters is the love you shared and the life you experienced as part of something real, beyond your understanding, that will continue after you're gone. *That's* your legacy. You're living it.

With billions of stars in our galaxy, and billions of galaxies, one person's physical contribution on planet Earth is zero. This is not to say they didn't profoundly impact others' lives. While a person's contributions may reverberate for ages in various ways, they will mostly do so quietly and without recognition or thanks. So do things because they reflect who you are, not for a certain outcome. Let outcomes take care of themselves.

In billions of years, there will be no life on Earth. How's your legacy doing?

After a few generations, no one can know you. They won't remember. In one hundred years, you'll be a name on a family tree. Of course, how often do you think of your great-grandparents? You didn't know them. Does it matter to you what some great guy named Dave did in 1751? He was a prominent doctor and very successful. He was a big deal. Do you care? And in the scope of time, 1751 was just a moment ago. Dave, along with everyone he ever knew, are on a hill somewhere, quiet.

What mattered in his life? Moments. Experiences. The exploration of "who you are."

Can you name a celebrity from 1744? At most, you'll mention a historical figure that exists only in books. But it's a name; that's it. That name, to you, is the response to a trivia question or answer on a grade-school history test. In other words, you don't know them as people.

How has the "legacy" of someone, even a king or queen, from 1580 truly impacted your life? Even if they had some sort of impact felt generations later, you wouldn't know it. To know it, it's got to be inside your bubble.

Would you say a monarch has a substantial legacy? Yes? So, what were Queen Victoria's contributions to your life? How has she impacted you, not peripherally but specifically? How often do you think about her? How much do you care? She's no one; she's a name and nothing more.

Most people walk the very thin tightrope between great feelings of worth and worthlessness and, if they grew up famous, haven't developed the intrapersonal skills or perspective that comes with experiencing both sides of fame.

When a celebrity dies, the public mourns. Who are they mourning? They are mourning a perception. How could it be otherwise? They don't know that person. If ten people die in a plane crash and one is famous, the only person the public mourns is the famous person. They "knew" them. But beyond mourning the humanity in someone, how could they mourn a person they didn't know?

If awards, titles, accolades, and fame result from your work, great. And you're still you. If nothing results from your work, great. And you're still you.

Imagine if, suddenly, you were on a deserted island with nothing. Who would you be? Would you still be a lawyer or a cashier? Would being "pretty" mean something to you when no one cares because there's no one to care?

Being grateful for what you already have is the surest pathway to peace.

# CHAPTER FIVE

# Life in a Bubble:

## *Your Relationship with the World*

*Chase after the truth like all hell and you'll free
yourself, even though you never touch its coat tails.*

**—CLARENCE DARROW**

> **Lessons from Near Death:**
>
> *Take (and give) opinions with a grain of salt. Your
> worldview is unimaginably small, so you never have
> a complete picture. Reserve the right to change
> your mind. If you can't detach from your need to
> be right, you'll never know what's real, and it will
> own you.*

## REDUCING THE WORLD TO WHAT'S FAMILIAR

Busyness is made more manageable by creating a silo—a bubble by which most people view life defined by its degree of relevance to *them*, suns of their own universes.

By reducing the world to a bubble, it becomes theirs. Their experience, mostly made up of daily routines and piecemeal information of a world they've never personally explored, is easier to compartmentalize, understand, manage, and control. As such, they have many opinions of a world they know little about. And rather than accepting this and opening their minds to learning, they double down on beliefs critical to identities they've created so they can feel okay in their bubbles.

Most people think this tiny bubble is reflective of the real world as a whole. It's the womb for all the biases of familiarity that shape their perceptions of life outside it. Everyone should be a Republican because they are. Everyone needs Christianity because they do.

Their bubble is about as big as their neighborhood, the places they frequent, and their social media accounts, which, along with a single source of biased television news commentary, are where they get all their information about the outside world.

A person's average day is getting the kids off to school, grabbing a coffee, going to work, picking up the kids, going home for dinner, and settling in for a night in front of the television and social media. It's mundane but busy, and there are lots of fires to fight—rambunctious kids, laundry, meals, bills. These routines become a person's ingrained circuitry.

Do something over and over again, and soon you won't have to think about it. Your thoughts are overrun with commentary about a past that's gone or a future that hasn't happened yet. As your mind becomes hardwired, unused mental connections fade away—a process called synaptic pruning. In other words, familiarity in thoughts and behaviors shapes future thoughts and behaviors because they take over your world.

Most people stay close to their social group, their workplace, and their sphere of influence. In their bubble, they think in terms not of how they relate to others but of how others relate to them. In other words, their worldview is really their perception of how others view them—how they fit in their worlds.

In a bubble, everything's a crisis, every problem big, every gossip dramatic. It's exhausting. The size of everything in a bubble is made larger as the world around someone proportionally shrinks to fit them.

Many people will complain of the overpriced latte while countless others in the world pray for water. They'll post a picture (on social media) of themselves enjoying a mimosa and are confident others will find this important news. Religion, politics, world events, or social media ramblings—most people will have an opinion on those things but don't seek out the larger context. Other points of view don't fit into their bubbles in ways that can be understood, controlled, and managed without feeling threatened by them.

Someone's life may be uncomfortable, but it's familiar, so they often stay in it—a job they hate or a relationship that's toxic. They can control and manage those things because at least they know them. Sure, people can be "happy" in their bubbles, but it's circumstantial. They are happy until *this* or *that* happens—the car is repossessed, or they're laid off. In their bubbles, emotions are a roller coaster of ups and downs, reflecting things that happen *to* them. For most people, life is spent waiting for these things—relationships, cars, money, roles—that "make them happy."

True happiness is not circumstantial. It's not a state of mind. It's not a fleeting joy that comes and goes with the fulfillment of wants. It's not a mood. You can encounter adversity or an unhappy emotion and still be a happy person. That's why so few people experience it for any lasting time. They will never find it because they're often looking for it in a role.

In a bubble, there's a religious quality to an opinion. Opinions are extensions of yourself. Your viewpoint is right because it's yours. Choose a topic: abortion, politics, capital punishment, gun control, sexuality, gender, religion, or which dog breed is best. The surest sign someone is secure in themselves (or not) is how they communicate with people who disagree.

Disagreements escalate when people become threatened. Any perceived threat to their identity—gender, sexual orientation, nationality, or otherwise—triggers a reaction in the other. What's threatened, exactly?

The truth? No, you are. When you're offended, what you mean is that you're threatened.

When an argument comes to a head and the emotional defenses subside, each person occasionally realizes they were completely controlled by those feelings before falling back into autopilot. "I'm sorry about what I said. I didn't mean that." It will happen again and again because they don't understand how this works.

Over time, people develop tunnel vision as they seek only the information that supports what they already believe, so each day, they're inundated with viewpoints that match their own and won't consider others. Liberals digest liberal news, and conservatives digest conservative news, for example.

When developing an opinion about an issue, the most intelligent thing someone can think or say is, "This is my opinion that I believe is reasonable because it's based on credible facts and multiple perspectives. I'm open to hearing all sides of the issue because I'm not tied to an outcome or threatened by being wrong. When I discover additional information, I reserve the right to change my opinion. Being right or wrong has no bearing on my value. I'm simply seeking what's true."

We have too much confidence in our own viewpoints. Reserve the right to change your mind. Overconfidence makes people ignorant. Suspend judgment. In any situation, or upon encountering any piece of news, consider two questions: Were you there? What information do you actually have?

"Diversity" also means diversity of opinions. When someone says their company is "diverse," they don't know what that means. Just because two people are of a different race doesn't mean they get to check the diversity box. Diversity means different, varied backgrounds, personalities, family situations, experiences, and, of course, opinions that they can be open to discovering. But if opinions differ from theirs, suddenly they're not on board like they were when they thought the definition of diversity wasn't so . . . diverse.

## RAISED THAT WAY

Saying you were "raised that way" is never a good reason to believe something if you're interested in what's actually true. Nor is tradition. "True to you" isn't truth. The truth is in the questioning.

I once overheard a group of three janitors during a break in the atrium of the office building in which we worked. They were all on their phones, scrolling through their social media, each commenting about the headlines, mostly about politics. Without considering the source or facts, and without actually reading the articles, it was clear their outspoken opinions were swayed effortlessly by the headlines alone and how those media portrayals fit into their already-held beliefs.

So many people can't think critically about what they're seeing. Most Americans (two-thirds), for example, can't name all three branches of government, but 100 percent of them have opinions about how the government should be run.

Make up a headline, and watch people believe it. Gravitating toward others like themselves, these janitors shared the same general beliefs as those in their bubbles. Each janitor commented, reinforcing each other's opinions and, in doing so, cultivating feelings of mutual belongingness.

People also tend to believe what they hear if it supports their identity, even if it isn't necessarily part of their own personal experience, and, without verification, adopt those things as parts of themselves.

For example, if you convince someone they're a "victim," they will be a victim; you've planted that seed. They will then only see information that supports that belief.

When someone creates their identity as a "victim," they will sometimes shout it from the mountaintops. "*That's* who I am." They can find satisfaction and power in feeling "courageous" or "brave." Some may enjoy having those terms hurled at them a thousand times a day as they bask in feelings of heightened significance as a sort of tragic hero.

Alone on a deserted island, there are no victims.

I once knew a woman who was a "victim" of sexual assault. Everyone (her social media "friends") knew she had been sexually assaulted but knew little else. Empathic to her, they assumed the assault involved rape or some other heinous act; they didn't know she was simply smacked on the rear by a drunk patron at a local bar. Was that behavior appropriate? No, but does it have the same implications as other behaviors? No. But who would ask? Once someone becomes a label, few would question it.

People make assumptions when they read headlines—when they read labels. "Victim" is what she created herself to be because of what it got her: validation. If she didn't need to be a victim, she wouldn't be a victim.

This doesn't mean nothing terrible has happened to a person. But the moment you say, "I'm *that*," then that's what you are. And you will seek validation to make it true and, often, to soothe.

Again, *you* get to choose how you show up in the world. You're not a label unless you decide to be a label. And that's what people will believe without exploring beyond it. Most people don't ask questions. They are even less likely to ask questions if they're in groups. That's the power of influence—when someone can tap into a platform to sway people in masses by controlling labels. Powerful people know how to manipulate groups that won't question things that they might as individuals.

How do these powerful people do this? They use the media. Media is not merely a mirror on society; it is an actor upon it—a showcase of all the pitfalls of personal, career, and business interests that are so entertaining. What you see in the media is a heavily distorted curation of other people's opinions that dictate yours without your knowledge. It's framing, getting sucked into a narrative—facts molded to fit opinions. And what's a fact but a relative opinion about what's factual? You just have to believe it.

As a young server only weeks removed from college, I brought a middle-aged, seemingly affluent businesswoman a Maker's Mark cocktail.

"This doesn't taste quite right. It's not Maker's Mark. Take it back," she said with a grimace as she held up her glass.

"I'm so sorry. I'll get that corrected right away," I said before returning it to the bartender.

"It's right. Just take it back to her," the bartender said.

"What?! But—"

"Just do it. Watch," the bartender said.

So I took *the exact same drink* back to the table. "Sorry about that, ma'am," I said as I placed the glass on the table.

She took a sip. "Perfect! Thank you so much!"

It all starts with the framing.

Before the internet, people knew little. They had newspapers and just a couple of television news stations to rely on for news. Since the internet, they know lots of things; it's just impossible for them to know what's true because there's such an insane competition for their attention that the truth becomes pliable for the sake of enticing viewers.

To have an opinion that's true, you've got to open yourself to your own blind spots and venture outside of what's familiar. You have to look at opposing viewpoints, or else all you have is half a story that you constantly reaffirm with a steady stream from a single source. If you're an old, white, conservative male and all you watch is Fox News talk shows, for example, you're probably never going to get any other story than the one that fits you. It's rarely the full story in its full context.

We fill in the gaps on our own. You've got to question things and seek out what's reasonable. It won't come to you.

*It don't matter who you hear it from;*
*it's the same story.*

**—EDWARD NORTON (AS AARON STAMPLER)**
**IN *PRIMAL FEAR***

Yesterday I watched half a prime-time news segment on CNN. I then switched to watch the rest of the hour on Fox News, two networks that typically represent starkly different political ideologies. I laughed at the absurdity of how I could be watching news of the same event, yet their framing was *opposite*.

When I switched to Fox News, a Republican network, a doctored graphic of the president, a Democrat, appeared on the screen. In it, he had red eyes, horns, and other devil-like features. *Who's doing the graphics here?* I thought. This is "professional news," no? Who can say there's no bias in *that*?

When a segment headline (at the bottom of the screen) reads "Dems work to silence free speech," how many ways are viewers going to take that when they already believe a certain way? No one is going to delve deeper on a topic when they've already decided to believe whatever's on the screen. There's more to a story than six words and one viewpoint. But it doesn't matter what the story is; the framing is all you need.

How many people do you know who consistently watch two contrasting news networks? You've got two choices, or parties, in politics, regardless of how many parties there actually are. How do you remain open to the truth?

Self-awareness is an essential start. However, for most people, self-awareness is proportional to the size of their bubble. Who knew that Diane the deli clerk, who has never left her neighborhood, would become so informed on politics and world events simply by scanning the headlines in her social media feed?

Maybe you know a neighbor, relative, or friend who's quick to offer fiery opinions on the day's hot topics, religion, or politics and is quick to engage others on those issues. Often, it's a struggle to get a word in, debate, or disagree without them becoming defensive.

> *No one ever thinks they're stupid.*
> *It's part of the stupidity.*
>
> **—ROBERT F. COLESBERRY**

So, who are you? If you're not roles, titles, or accolades, are you your opinions?

No, you aren't those either. Opinions are mostly just an amalgamation of thoughts that reflect feelings. Again, most people don't do their due diligence to seek complete information. It just has to be true enough to be agreeable. And for most, it's not enough to believe something; they have to make someone else believe it too.

I once attended a trade show that lined the streets of a small town. All sorts of activities and vendors filled tents as far as the eye could see down Main Street. There were funnel cakes, local artists, and all kinds of handmade household items.

Standing beside an artist's tent, an older woman commented on a piece.

"That one is beautiful," she said to me.

I'm usually not one to become drawn into long conversations, but she was pleasant. We chatted about the gorgeous hiking trails in the area and the variety of artwork that depicted truly breathtaking scenery. After about half an hour of talking, things shifted.

From her shoulder bag, she withdrew a small pamphlet and placed it in my hands.

"Where do you go to church?" she asked.

*Here we go . . .* I thought.

For the next thirty minutes, she spoke continuously about her beliefs and why I needed to hear them. To some, this may be "The Good News." But I couldn't help but feel that throughout our entire conversation, she had an agenda—hers. This became more evident as, after an hour, she grew a bit frustrated with me as I became more closed. I felt duped. I felt like a means to an end. I left, politely thanking her for the conversation.

So what if I disagreed? What if I was secure in my own beliefs that were different from hers? Were we no longer friends? Would she think I was just "lost"? What in her was frustrated? Based on our conversation, I knew that she was born and raised in that small town and that she never left. So what makes her truth so much truer? The fact that she believes it.

Suppose I had much the same intentions. What if, at the moment she withdrew her pamphlet from her bag, I withdrew one of my own . . . for *Scientology?* How would that have changed the dynamic of the conversation?

"It's faith," many people say. They were "raised that way."

This is not to say that any belief is untrue, but what makes it true other than your believing it is? All the "evidence," right? The facts? Or your view of them?

Faith doesn't make something reasonable. Otherwise, you could believe any sort of thing, like your toaster is sacred and can transport you to other dimensions. Dare someone to disprove it. If reason is important to you, then you'll ask questions. Then what you're saying when you believe something is that you've asked enough questions to find that faith reasonable.

Or reason isn't important to you in faith, and so the truth isn't either. In that case, you must have been raised with everyone around you telling you their opinions of the truth. For a while, Santa Claus was very real, until he wasn't. Your decision to believe is all that's required to make something true. You *need* it to be true.

For most of human existence, there was little differentiation between *story* and *history.* History *was* story. What was widely considered true was driven by oral tradition. While there has since been a shift through science, most of what exists today is a hodgepodge of traditions, stories, and facts all thrown in the pot. The taste, however, is specific to a person. Each tastes something different, and no one asks about the ingredients.

People can't handle the "I don't knows." Uncertainty doesn't provide comfort. It doesn't fit into their bubbles where everything is understood, controlled, and managed. There's power in saying "I don't know" or "I can't know."

Instead, we raise our kids believing a narrative—a very storybook, childish understanding of religion. We don't discuss the arguments or deeper philosophical underpinnings that make belief reasonable. It's never addressed at any age.

There is a certain maturity required to make choices about what's true about the universe beyond the fact you told them so. If *you* are open, you can allow your children that same openness so they can explore what's reasonable to them.

Instead, kids in diapers are being "saved" with things like baptism and countless other rituals or belief systems that are thrust upon them without any real choice. When a kid is baptized, they don't know what that means. You have made one of life's most profound choices for them. Luckily, they've found the truth because Mom and Dad had it handy for them and will push it on them for the next few decades. Who do they pray to at the dinner table? Have you ever listened to an eight-year-old pray? They pray for their wants—an easier path and blessings for themselves and friends, as if wishing upon their own personal genies.

So many teenagers behave like normal teens with all the drama, pettiness, and self-centeredness that comes with teen hormones, and I wonder, *That person embodies those teachings?* But the teachings aren't made real quite yet. These teens are checking the boxes of belief because Mom or Sunday school said so. They showed up, so it counts. Ask them and of course they'll profess they *are* their label. "I'm a Christian," they say. "I'm excited to see what God has in store for me!" I often hear. Or "Whatever God wills." "Whatever God wants for my life."

Go to a religious university and absolutely everything you do and study is predicated on already knowing your religion as fact. In an institute of higher learning in which questioning is integral to learning, questioning is exactly what they *don't* do. In other words, you enter these religious universities thinking that specific belief is actually true and not just a part of your identity.

So, of all the religions in the world, you thought about what makes the most reasonable sense, and you made *that* choice? How did you arrive at that choice? Or perhaps you don't believe in a literal sense. In that case, you really don't believe it at all, but you haven't separated from it or ventured into other possibilities because it's so much a part of your identity since birth.

People aren't defending their religions; they're defending *themselves.*

Perhaps you're offended. What offends you, specifically? The words? Because they're questioning? Are you offended because I'm questioning what's true to you? Does it make a difference to the truth if I question it? Or if you do? Why does it make a difference to you what I question? Why does it matter if I disagree? Does that cause discomfort in you? Anger? Why? Why don't you ever ask "Why?"

Offense is the pain of vulnerability when realness becomes shaky.

We assume the afterlife is a sensory experience because we long for it; it's familiar. We can't consider the possibility that what's beyond our time on earth is not a sensory experience at all but instead incomprehensible. After we die, we want all our greatest desires manifested, and we can't understand that it's beyond all that. To explain life in our bubbles so clearly and make it familiar, we have reduced God to, basically, a human with powers—human form, human emotion, even pettiness. He *needs* to be worshiped and praised. Doing so sways us into His good graces.

Earth is a speck of dust barely visible from our closest neighbor, let alone in an incomprehensible universe, yet it conveniently fits right into our system of beliefs. If there is alien life, they can follow Jesus too. Perhaps they'll enjoy a pamphlet.

> *There are over 5,000 gods being worshiped by humanity. But don't worry . . . only yours is right.*
>
> **—ZACH BRAFF**

The Greeks, Romans, and countless other cultures believed what we now call "myths." We even study them with a smirk and chuckle at their clearly silly beliefs we can't imagine they thought were true. We think they're stories like any other—Zeus, Ares, Apollo. Zeus, the king, is the one with the flowing white beard that throws lightning bolts.

Well, that's still *us*; we're the same people that believed that stuff. The animal and people sacrifices, the witchcraft, Lord Xenu (Scientology), the golden Egyptian plates translated by seer stones (Mormonism), and so on—us, us, and us. They were raised that way, too.

If you're born in India, you're Hindu. If you're born in the Middle East, you're Muslim. If you're born in the United States, you're Christian. How likely is it that a baby growing up in Pakistan chooses Scientology? Pretty unlikely. That baby will grow up in its bubble, with everyone inside it telling him "the truth."

*This* is truth in a bubble. It's everything encompassed therein that's true because it fits your understanding of what's true without deviation. We see what we want to see. Ask a world traveler or combat soldier about the real world. Your world isn't it.

More people have killed for God than any other reason, all for their rightness in making others wrong. Many "righteous" people have committed some of the worst atrocities imaginable. It's easier to kill if it's "for God." They're right because it's them, and God is on their side. They've got all that grace. If something good happens, it's because God has bestowed blessings upon them. If something bad happens, God is teaching a lesson, or it's because He "works in mysterious ways."

No one believes themselves "bad"; they just "made mistakes." Bad people go to Hell, and good people go to Heaven. You, of course, are good. You are going to a place of puffy white clouds and angels playing harps to reunite with everyone you love, exactly like you thought. You've found the truth of the universe, coincidentally at the precise moment you needed it because in prison what else do you have? You have to do what you have to do to feel okay.

Again, don't worry; your beliefs are all true.

A football coach thinks it's a good call if it's in his favor. Otherwise, it's an injustice.

Or when your kid misbehaves at school, "It's not my kid. He wouldn't do that." Yes, he would. And when something's happening *to* your kid, you can't figure out how another parent could be so unaware.

No one believes themselves promiscuous; they're just "expressing themselves," "haven't found the right person," or are "playing the field."

No one believes themselves a liar; it was always "for a good reason," or the other person pushed them into it.

No boss thinks *they* are the problem in a toxic work culture; it's everyone else. The military, for example, is known to "make leaders," not necessarily hire them. But you can't make someone have self-awareness.

On a resume, you're a "team player" or "people person." Who would say otherwise? Who sees themselves otherwise?

Elections are "rigged," despite zero evidence, and only when your preferred politician loses. Or it's all a conspiracy. When they win, it's fair and square. *That* election was fine.

It's only unequal if you're the victim of the inequality—on the receiving end. I've never heard a man complain of too much pay, for example. Again, it's only unequal if you are the victim of it.

Similarly, there is no racism if you haven't experienced it. Ask an old, white, retired, upper-middle-class, conservative man, and he'd be hard-pressed to see it. Or if you have experienced it, it sometimes seems everyone's a racist.

You're against immigration unless you're an immigrant. Would you not do anything for your family?

Free speech is paramount at any cost—one of those inalienable rights . . . unless you say something other people disagree with. Then, pipe down. But just because you *can* say something doesn't mean you should or that it's intelligent, respectful, or appropriate. It also doesn't entitle you to silence or to bulldoze others in the process. There's a time and place. And there's something called "dialogue" that few understand.

Certainly, you have the right to exercise free speech any time you choose to do so. Anyone *could* do anything they choose, although that choice is almost always predicated on the presumption that other people care to know your opinion at all times and that every time must be an appropriate time to voice those opinions because they're yours.

Of course, your speech may be about what's "right," according to you, and any forum is appropriate simply because you choose it. Realize, though, as you complain about an injustice, that you have the ability to complain about it at all, publicly, *at work*—as a professional athlete, for example, while you make millions of dollars to the detriment of the business that pays you. In business, business owners just don't want the circus as you protest as a champion of your beliefs. Why? Because it divides.

Many millionaire athletes are champions of great causes. They fight for justice, even if their league hemorrhages fans, and cash, as a result. But when it comes time to negotiate a contract, they're all about that business.

To be heard, you have to relate to people. You have to understand them and draw them together. You have to connect. When you vilify "the others," you have closed that door. It becomes easier to hate someone when you feel hated. And when you hate, the issues don't matter; you're not listening, and you don't care to listen.

*There are two wolves fighting inside of all of us.*
*The first one is evil, the second one is good.*
*Which wolf will win? The one you feed.*

**—NATIVE AMERICAN PROVERB**

Do you want change? Okay, be precise; that's where the progress is. Let's have a specific, civil dialogue. Offer *solutions*. Help people help you. Often, one person doesn't know what they can do. You can't attack and judge and call it open dialogue. Accusing strangers you have never met of something ugly will not build bridges. Resentment builds by shoveling people into a category and calling them oppressors.

Protestors that don't offer specific solutions are just that: protestors. And all they'll ever do is protest. Instead, help people understand. Otherwise, it's just venting—a collective emotional catharsis that will amount to nothing.

If you become violent, and especially if bystanders are impacted along the way, not only will your message fall on deaf ears, but you've tarnished it. You've driven away any listeners, and now they're angry *and* not listening. Then, you'll become angrier and more violent, dumbfounded as to why no one's listening. And you've become more repulsive.

You're not going to get very far generalizing and pointing fingers at people who are saying, "That's not me." They're not going to listen. And many times, it's not them, per se; it's the outliers who are reacting most negatively. But you *do* need them for the dialogue; it's just that people who are judging you are so hard to talk to. If you seek to understand people who are unlike you, you will learn about a world you can't see. Seeking to understand is a good thing, but it has to be from both sides. People have to feel like they can chat freely with someone who won't nail them to a cross and destroy their lives. Otherwise, it's easier to not talk about it.

The only reasonable opinion is yours. The only right religion is the one you believe. The only real language is the one you speak. The best team is the one you are on. The greatest country is yours; its founding fathers were infallible. Whoever is on "the other side" of your opinion is "uneducated" or "ill informed." Not you, though.

You're saying the same things as "the others," though probably not as intended (on opposite sides). Again, in a bubble of familiarity, we see what we want to see—what we need to see.

The Dunning-Kruger Effect is an excellent illustration of our blind spots whereby people of lower ability are unable to sense their lower ability and understanding and so overestimate it because their ability is low. Whereas people of higher ability are unable to sense their higher ability and understanding, and similarly underestimate it because their ability is high.

We just can't see ourselves.

CHAPTER SIX

# More Time Tomorrow:

## *Your Relationship with Time*

❖

**Lessons from Near Death:**

*Most people spend their time in thoughts of the past or future. Nothing you do will change your relationship with time unless you change the way you see it.*

❖

## THE ILLUSION

We never think this is all the time we'll have, or this is as old as we'll ever get.

Christine, a former client, was frequently overextended and, of course, stressed. She was a student, pastor, full-time counselor, and military reservist. Each day, she lived by a strict timeline and under the general belief that once graduate school ended and she retired from the military in six months, things would be better. And so, for those six months, she lived on that to-do list, waiting to reach its end, ready to receive her prize: more time.

I'm often dumbfounded when individuals remark that they've purposely spent all of their twenties and thirties working on their careers. What's often meant is that work becomes the focal point of their existence. They sacrifice the present in the assumption they have a million tomorrows in which to find themselves.

Yes, be "stable." What does that mean? Yes, make choices so you can keep food on the table and a roof over your head. But where does it stop? Do you have a point at which you will have enough so you can live? Have you defined that point? For most, when they find more—more money, titles, roles, cars—they want more. They *become* more. Give a child a cookie, and they'll want two.

Once school ended and military retirement came, an ecstatic Christine took a vacation and thanked the heavens for such relief. She felt it for a while, yet a strange discomfort persisted. Then, over the next several weeks, as she returned to work, we both noticed that her busyness also seemed to return. The relief was gone.

She wondered, *How is this possible?* How could she be so busy without the high demands of schoolwork or military duties? In fact, Christine was even busier than before! Her new job and life seemed to expand to fill her capacity, and without concrete boundaries, she took on too much. It wasn't long before she was overwhelmed again, more confused than before. And she wasn't happier. Her confusion stemmed from her surprise that the busyness seemed to happen so quickly and without her knowing, as if she woke up one day overwhelmed again. It happened *to* her.

It doesn't matter how busy someone is on paper or to an outsider; the stress, the overwhelming busyness, snowballs and always fills a person's capacity to handle it. They feel it long before they see it—when they're already experiencing adverse effects in their life.

*Work expands so as to fill the*
*time available for its completion.*

**—PARKINSON'S LAW**

Christine couldn't see her inability to create real boundaries. She was successful, decorated, educated, and intelligent. Her inability has nothing to do with any of these things.

Despite her extensive education and training, her solution was always more of the same—trudging through, waiting. Again, we always see others more easily than ourselves. We can't always see how we spend our time.

I found the lack of boundaries that Christine experienced a familiar story during sessions. Many people have difficulty saying "no" to others, to obligations, to demands in which they don't realize they have a choice to make for themselves in order to live well. Remember, you're the guardian of your energy, and no one will guard it for you.

You may take on responsibilities for other people. Helping others is a great thing, but how helpful will you be at the expense of your own well-being? As you're reminded before a flight, you must always take the oxygen first. *Then* you help others, or else you're part of the group that needs help; you're part of the panic.

One who struggles to create real boundaries with their time will sometimes feel guilty for not helping loved ones, friends, or colleagues. Such is the case even when other commitments prevent them from doing so. They can't help but feel bad about it. Helping is how they build value. *That's* their identity. That's how they feel self-worth. They're the person who helps. If they can't, who are they? Nobody.

Some of my most stressed clients had the least to do and vice versa. They always perceived themselves to be busy, regardless of how busy they actually were. This tendency is usually inherent in personality. They feel busy, so they must be busy. It was easy to think, *You have no kids, no job, and sleep till noon. How busy are you? What do you do all day?* But, again, they can't see themselves, and their time slips away somewhere.

Many people desire change but are unwilling to do the things that create change. Instead, they often wait for change to happen *to* them; they can't see their role in it. They chase the dangling carrot only to discover they're the one dangling it.

They may go to therapy or "read all the books," but what's it actually going to take? This busyness isn't in their head; *they* are in their head, and some people attract busyness as if they have their own gravity.

What happens when you make suggestions to someone who wants change but doesn't want to do anything to create it? You get a long list of reasons why it won't work. They have to complete this or that task before change is possible. Change will come tomorrow. Something always has to happen before they're ready.

You'll start eating healthy and exercising when the kids' soccer season ends. When you're done with your work assignment, you'll finally pick up that paint brush that once provided so much joy. That was many years ago.

There is no perfect "ready." There are always things to do. Accept that. You have to live *in* that. So, what's worth your time?

The passage of time becomes blurry. I once had a client who frequently started sessions by listing all the tasks she had to complete before she was ready to change—the tasks that prevented her from doing what she said she would do *today*. She couldn't see that she was no further along than years ago and that doing the same things wasn't going to get her anywhere. The tasks changed, but she did not.

Time always seems slow in the moment—the workday, the workweek, the meeting, the wait at the doctor's office. You try to speed through those things that seem to creep by so slowly toward relief. But with clarity in hindsight, you will view your time differently. What seems slow today will always seem like a flash when looking back.

Trading away even one week, one month, or one year is a big decision and should not be taken lightly. The older you get, the faster time seems to go by. You'll wish you did more during those healthy years that you traded away for a few fleeting pleasures, or worrying, or wishing things were different.

What did you do with that time? You were in your thoughts—in the past or future. Nonacceptance is the willingness to carry a burden *forever*.

Humans are the only species on earth to live almost exclusively in the past or future—pain or anxiety. No animal thinks about how it was wronged twelve years ago or what it must do next Thursday. There is no self-pity. My blind cat does not spend her days lamenting the fact that she's blind.

We pine over the past to rectify it. If we can't change the past, maybe we can twist our perception of it. We also spend much of our lives seeking "closure," which we think will free us of the past. Closure is just an idea—the belief that you can change the past by analyzing it enough. It's really just finding the right justifications to let go.

All that it takes to let go of past pain is the decision not to feed it with your energy—not to get into the weeds mulling over things you can't change and compounding one mistake with others because you're too stubborn to think otherwise.

Consider a relationship that has ended abruptly. Bad breakups can sometimes haunt someone forever. Relationships end because, ultimately, at least one person has decided they no longer find the other a good match. Maybe they just don't like you. You might agree with the reasons, or you might not. What does it really matter? They don't want to be with you any longer.

It matters to you because the reason affects your perception of yourself and your worth. Often, for closure, the person who was broken up with wants their former partner's "reasons" for the breakup so they can make sense of them—so they can reconcile the vulnerability of being someone that wasn't "good enough" to be wanted.

Maybe it's a good reason, or maybe it's not. Maybe you smell. Maybe there's no reason other than that they found someone better (until they're not) or newer (until they're not). Maybe you said something (that caused an emotional reaction in them). Maybe you're a jerk. Maybe they are. Maybe they're bored. Maybe you're too familiar, so they can no longer create themselves into the person they want to be. You don't "make them happy."

What does it really matter? You are still you, and their reasons have no bearing.

Do you want closure? What most people mean when they say they want closure is that they want to fully reconcile the loss of not just a person but also feelings of diminishment. They will rationalize every reason for the breakup until they're convinced of their own worth so those reasons no longer hurt.

Some people never get to the point of acceptance (or healing) because the pain is rehashed every time they think about it; no rationalization has ever been convincing enough for them to feel okay. Again, nonacceptance is the willingness to carry something forever. Closure is the art of making something an easier pill to swallow.

Most of the time, people don't love each other for "who they are" anyway. How can they? They don't know who they themselves are. Mostly, when they say, "I love you," they're saying they love the fulfillment you provide them until you don't. The success of a relationship is often determined by where someone derives their value, internally or externally.

Again, you will always have two choices: worry or not worry. No matter what you choose, worrying changes nothing.

The mind lives in worst-case scenarios. The vast majority of the time, situations don't unfold the way you think they will. They occur in ways you can't foresee. So, your worrying doesn't help, and again, if something doesn't help, it hurts.

One former client was a young woman who was incessantly worried. For six months, she spoke about how she would be stuck with additional duties at work when her boss went on maternity leave— duties she couldn't handle. For six months, she truly suffered, even entering into a depression. Her mind racing, she was unable to hear anything outside the noise. No other opinion changed hers. Then, like magic, her boss did *not* return, and thus the company was free to hire another full-time manager who turned out to be better. Given my client's willingness to help in her boss's absence, she received a raise. She couldn't believe it.

We had a long discussion about all the worrying, which was for naught, and she even laughed about it. And she had an epiphany; the worrying added nothing. Had she *not* worried, she could have prepared for any outcome just the same. She also would've had a better life at home with her husband and kids, rather than carrying all the stress and making herself and others miserable.

Never again, she decided, would she trade so much precious time worrying when it wasn't worth the cost.

Can *you* be okay with uncertainty? That's what worrying is—discomfort with uncertainty. You can prepare for things, sure, but you can never control them. Trust that you will respond, like always, with all the resolve you know is within you. Desired result or not, worrying won't make a difference.

Do you remember what you worried about one year ago? One week ago? No, you don't. Those worries are swallowed up by new ones—new crises on the to-do list that never ends.

It is one thing to worry *in* a situation, such as when swimming in the ocean and you see a great white shark rushing toward you; that's fear. But most worries are stories you create to control and know outcomes.

Living in the past and future, time slips by, and soon you realize where it went.

*Time is the ultimate illusion that you have more future to find yourself in.*

**—ECKHART TOLLE**

Most people will receive horrible health diagnoses at some point or another. What do they do? Like clockwork, they will reflect on their lives, do some "soul searching," rush to create bucket lists, meditate, find Jesus, and finally seek peace for the first time. It's a trauma that pulls you into a moment. But what if you have lived your whole life that way, outside your bubble?

In his book *The Black Swan*, Nassim Nicholas Taleb describes the "black swan theory" that refers to the biases that blind people to unexpected traumatic events and catastrophes that could have otherwise been predicted—a terrorist attack, shooting, bridge collapse, or pandemic that's rationalized in hindsight.

Such is the case after any traumatic event whereby you experience a newfound clarity until the shock wears away and you revert back to what's familiar. After a car accident, for example, you have a new lease on life . . . until you don't.

Your will to change is proportional to the extent something shocks you.

Often, we misjudge how frequently these events occur because, until they permeate your bubble's wall, it's just peripheral noise. But things happen all around you—car accidents, heart attacks, cancer, hurricanes. It just doesn't seem like it because, again, time seems slow in the moment, and we live life in our heads. We don't think these things can happen to us until they do. But they do happen to someone; collectively, they're not so rare, and one day that someone will be you.

Again, in a bubble, we see the world as it relates to us. The rest is noise. An event has to enter that bubble to be seen. If a person can't see their direct relationship to something, it's "not their problem." "The others will help." The horror of the earth is when everyone thinks that.

When someone tosses a cigarette butt in the gutter or throws a glass bottle in the trash, for example, they live in willful ignorance as if to say, "This doesn't affect me right now, and I don't see what impact this behavior has (so it must have none), and, thus, I don't care. Not my problem."

Droughts, wildfires, the shrinking of polar ice, or disease—it's not your problem. Climate isn't a problem until it enters your bubble. Conservation isn't a problem until it is; there are species alive now that your grandkids will only see in books. Disease isn't a problem until you're stricken with it.

Ask people if they care, and some will say yes. Some really do care about these things. But there are different degrees of caring. Some will care but do nothing. There's no time, and it wouldn't make a difference anyway. And they can't see when there will be time to care about those things. So they are spectators, waiting for better tomorrows, who watch the world without living in it.

Each year a mother goose builds her nest in the mulch on the median outside my office. I secretly wish she wouldn't make one there; it's too exposed. The median is in the middle of a massive parking lot, but thankfully she chooses a spot a good distance away from the building.

During the spring, she returns to that exact spot and median (which is amazing) and creates a raised mound from the mulch with a large divot in its center. I often wonder how far she's traveled and how she's able to find that exact spot every time.

I've watched her day after day, week after week, as she sat in the rain, the cold, and in the darkness, caring for her eggs. I sometimes walked to my car late in the evenings in an empty lot, and I could see her in the distance. I was careful to stay a respectful distance away. I once even warned a passerby that it wasn't a good idea to approach her as she did, and with so much bread. She gave me a strange look. First, that's not the way to feed her, nor is it healthy. It also made me sick to see, even from several feet away, a massive colony of ants surrounding the goose, attracted by all the junk. Even worse, that poor mother goose had to fend away large crows also attracted by the scraps. It was a heartbreaking sight.

The best thing to do for wild animals is to leave them alone.

Every spring, one day, instead of seeing her sitting there, I'd spot a whole mess of feathers and eggs broken open (not into). I always smile when I see a group of those cute, fuzzy little goslings trying to keep up with their mother.

But last year, on one of my particularly dizzy days, I returned to find the nest gone, buried by fresh mulch. The landscapers had either mulched over or discarded the eggs there only hours prior. Not their problem.

If we can't handle the little things, how can we handle the big ones? If you can't even manage to put your shopping cart back, what *else* can't you do? You're "busy." The rest is noise.

# CHAPTER SEVEN

# Letting Go:

## *The Small Stuff*

❖

### Lessons from Near Death:

*Feelings are like clouds; it's all weather. Just because you feel it doesn't make it true. Learn to understand why you feel a certain way by looking at those feelings and what information those feelings provide you about your state of mind. What do you gain by holding on to those feelings? What do you lose? If you do what most people do and pack all of your hurt and carry it on your back, your life will be sadly, unbearably heavy when it didn't have to be.*

❖

I f you become lost in small things, you, too, become small.

When you feel something, it's difficult to see beyond that feeling. You infer that feeling as the state of your life. You can't see the feeling will pass. You can't see a time before it, and you certainly can't see a time beyond it. And you make decisions that align with that feeling—sometimes with life-altering consequences.

Anything different than what you feel now seems an eternity away.

Change seems impossible. You can't see that change isn't an all-or-nothing proposition. In other words, you don't have to lose sixty pounds to see results. You'll see results after five, ten, and twenty pounds. Moment by moment, it will get easier. But, for now, you can't see your life beyond your current feelings about it. And because that's how you feel, the grass always looks greener on the other side of every fence.

Stick to the facts. Feelings aren't facts. They're (often irrational, knee-jerk) reactions to thoughts. Learn to observe them before you react.

"That's not true," a man says in an argument with his wife. "I don't have feelings for your friend." That may be a fact.

"But it's how I feel," his wife says as if that feeling makes it true. There are a number of questions she could ask herself: *Why do I feel this way? What do I actually know, not assume, about the situation? What are the facts? Are my feelings coming from elsewhere—feelings of jealousy or insecurity? From my past? Or are my feelings reasonable? Do they indicate a larger problem?*

"Letting go" is really the art of observation—the ability to look at your emotions, which is only possible if you detach from them. "Letting go" does not mean you no longer feel them, nor that you're unfeeling or cold. On the contrary, in detachment, you embrace emotions and can therefore make conscious choices about them. You understand them as reactions, so you don't automatically believe that your feelings reflect anything true without exploring them further. You take them with a grain of salt.

Observe your feelings by questioning them. Are they based on facts? What about them is real? Do you feel threatened in any way? What, exactly, is threatened? Why are you holding on to those feelings? What would make you let them go?

You can't "let go" of something you never had. "Letting go" is an idea of the mind. It implies something has to be actioned for you to allow the detachment. So "letting go" refers to a decision that arises after you observe and understand your emotions.

Imagine you're cut off in traffic. You want to give the other driver a "piece of your mind." Before you do, ask yourself, *Was it on purpose?*

*What do I actually know?* You don't know anything; you assume. Would knowing the driver was in a rush to the emergency room with his pregnant wife change your feelings about the situation? Could it have been an honest mistake? Maybe his wife left him. Maybe it was the worst day of his life. What will becoming angry change? How much of a difference did what happened truly make to your day? Why are you so angry? How will saying anything or carrying the anger around for the rest of the day help you or the situation?

If you say something to the other driver with a lot of anger, how will triggering defensiveness in them help? What lesson do you think you're teaching them? Do you ever make mistakes? You don't know it was on purpose. How would you feel if you had made the mistake?

Do you know how to defuse the situation? Why won't you? Because you've become the anger. Most people will never see a lesson to be learned because they're defensive. You can't ask these questions because you've already reacted to the situation. You didn't have time to look at it.

If you make someone wrong, they no longer hear you. Remember, you can't convince anyone of anything, least of all that they're wrong. Even if someone knows they're wrong, if they feel attacked, they will defend. They become an emotion—their armor. It can be impossible to reason with them. When they're venting, they're seeking relief and can be irrational in that moment.

Are they actually wrong, or are you hurt that they're right? What does it mean to be "hurt"? What makes them wrong? How do you know? Are you wrong? Can it be okay if you are? Again, you'll never ask these questions if you've already reacted. If you can ask the right questions, you're a step closer to what's actually true.

More importantly, how much energy is this reaction worth relative to the outcome? What did you think was going to happen when you reacted angrily? A tearful apology from a person who's "wrong"? There is no right or wrong in the world of emotion. There is only energy and how it's used. There are no winners in an argument. Your anger doesn't undo what's been done, so who are you punishing by holding on to that emotion? You're punishing yourself.

I once had a client who had held onto an intense anger for many years following a difficult breakup with an unfaithful partner.

"How does your anger and pain help you now?" I asked. "And how does your anger affect *him*? How are you punishing him with that anger?"

After a long pause, she replied, "I don't know . . ."

Maybe he's remorseful. Maybe he isn't. What difference does it truly make? She didn't need him to be remorseful to give herself permission to let go. *He* let go a long time ago. He was off someplace remarried and perhaps never giving her a second thought. The apology was lost in the mail. It always is. And how much energy, and life, did she exchange to carry that pain? Was it worth it?

We often carry pain as an unconscious need to right that wrong. But the other person isn't feeling that pain. In any situation, ask yourself, "What is the best possible action to yield the best possible outcome?" Stick to what's essential, and stay within your boundaries in terms of how you expend your energy. If there is nothing to gain by doing or saying something, let it go because it will only hurt *you*. Respond, don't react. Acknowledge your feelings; don't suppress them. Understand them. Letting go isn't something you have to do; there's pressure in that. It's something you allow.

"But *this* trauma happened to me. Am I supposed to just forget about it?" you might say.

Not at all. You don't have to do anything with it. Who says you have to? Look at it. How is it serving you? How is it helping you now? What's more painful, the event or the years-long mental commentary after the event as you constantly relive it?

Forgiveness has nothing to do with deserving. Forgiveness is something you do for you. No matter how long you relive a situation, you will never make someone sorry. And making someone sorry wouldn't make one bit of difference. Forgiveness is a decision you can make in an instant—when you decide something is not worth your energy.

*Forgiveness is the fragrance the violet sheds on the heel that has crushed it.*

**—ATTRIBUTED TO MARK TWAIN**

In any case, wouldn't the best "revenge" (which is, of course, meaningless) be to simply move on as if the other person no longer had power over you? You don't have one more moment for them.

Don't give any person power over your peace. Otherwise, your peace will always be contingent on just the right circumstances that are always in someone else's control, such as waiting on the wrongdoer's sincere apology that's lost in the mail.

They shouldn't have wronged you. But they did. Accept that. No amount of tears will make it otherwise. You will never "right the wrong." There's no way to do that. What you're looking for is the right set of conditions for you to reconcile what you've lost. But, again, you can't lose something you never really had. Make that person a pebble in your shoe, and then continue walking. *That's* power. *That's* quiet confidence. *That's* mighty.

Again, feelings aren't facts. Make no assumptions. Invent no stories, no commentary. When you're told something, just take it at face value and move on. Don't dwell. Don't make a life event your identity; it's something that happened to you but doesn't define you.

There is a vast difference between forgiving and forgetting. No one is asking you to forget. No one is asking you to pretend it never happened or to invite that person out for tea. But by separating the emotion from it, which no longer serves a purpose, you take back your power.

In some cases, it will be necessary to remove toxic people from your life. But you can forgive, and you can accept, for *you*.

*When people treat you like they don't care, believe them.*

**—AUTHOR UNKNOWN**

Be mindful of people and pain from the past that steal your energy. Forgiveness is something you do for yourself. What you can't forgive you end up becoming.

## GRIT

*Do not lose your knowledge that our proper estate is an upright posture, an intransigent mind and a step that travels unlimited roads. Do not let your fire go out, spark by irreplaceable spark, in the hopeless swamps of the approximate, the not-quite, the not-yet, the not-at-all.*

**—AYN RAND**

As they get older, most people grow out of dreams and into routines. They gravitate toward what's familiar because it's safe. They seek stability, confuse complacency for stability, and never venture far from their comfort zones.

How is it, then, that some people are able to move beyond the doubt, the fear, and the risk, away from the familiarity and into the unknown? What makes someone (an "ordinary" someone) decide one day to make a life-changing decision?

It's easy to look at someone who's successful and, without knowing how many failures they've experienced, think success comes easily. Sure, the grass seems greener, but you don't know how much manure they had to shovel to get there. No one ever achieved anything great without first taking some sort of risk and, most often, failing. A lot.

What type of person signs up for more failure? A glutton for punishment? A crazy person? An idiot? No, just someone who views their life (and their time here) differently.

First, a successful person sees risks as opportunities for learning. It's a way of being. Whether an outcome is favorable or not, they learn and move on. In other words, they've mastered the art of letting go. They focus on doing the "right things" and separate from the outcomes. They live in moments, not tomorrows. Failing doesn't make them a failure. It has nothing to do with who they are. They treat everything like one big experiment.

Without attachment to an outcome, the risk (to self-worth) disappears. So does the fear. Not only does failing not make you a failure, it's in fact *vital* to success. All those who are successful have failed at some point or another.

Second, successful people can tune out the noise—the internal dialogue, the distractions, the naysayers. They take opinions with a grain of salt. Ironically, most of the people in your life that have an opinion about what you should do have never been in your situation. Their fear will pull you back to the familiar. They may love you, but their advice comes from a place of worry.

Do you have a big idea? Do you hesitate to tell people? Why? Because you want to live in possibilities first, and people will always pull you into their fear.

A good way to address your fear about a big decision is to look at it logically and in its worst case. Look at it as an observer. If the worst that can happen becomes okay, what happens to the fear? You didn't get that job. So?

Living in worst-case scenarios, we look for virtual guarantees of success before taking the biggest risks. Most people have no stomach for failure. One failure, and they're done. Often, fear can become so great that we create self-fulfilling prophecies, meaning that we sabotage our own progress (*guaranteeing* failure) and confirm our already held beliefs that we were right all along as victims of life.

"I should've known this wouldn't work."

"I should've known she was out of my league."

"I'm no good. I'm a loser."

Is that how a confident person would talk?

Make the worst okay. If the worst does happen, which is unlikely, you will recover, and life will go on. Think of it this way: If you keep trying, it's likely that at some point, you will achieve your goal, although in ways you can't see right now. It's the law of averages. If you knew, for example, that in just six months you would discover a fantastic, life-changing opportunity, would all the failures be worth it? Most people would say "Yes," but, for now, *not* knowing is too much to bear. They're not focused on moments but tomorrows—on becoming something that "makes them happy." Let tomorrow take care of itself. For now, settle into doing the "right" things in the moment, one foot in front of the other.

No one plans to fail. But most people stand in their own way without knowing it.

Complacency happens when we give up hope. You will never see success unless you're okay with failure. We all feel like frauds at some point, and your feelings about it prove you right or wrong. Ultimately, you have to love yourself enough to let rejection be okay. You've got to decide it doesn't matter how many rejections you get. You are who you are, which is enough, and you let the cards fall where they may.

When you're rejected, it's not a rejection of you. A rejection could have occurred for any number of reasons, perhaps none of which have anything to do with you. Never assume.

If you applied for a job and didn't get a callback, how do you know they didn't have someone already in mind? How do you know you didn't apply at the end of a hiring cycle after all interviews had already been completed? Or maybe it was your resume format. You don't know; you assume.

Or maybe it *was* you. So? Adjust and move on. Maybe you just got beat. If there are eight hundred applicants for a job and you're one of the final two, one of those people still gets rejected. No one thinks a salutatorian is a "loser," but they still didn't finish first. Would you feel better knowing you were number two rather than number seven hundred forty-five? Again, you just don't know.

In any case, it doesn't make any difference to who you are. So stop analyzing it. Stop adding to the noise. The negative self-talk isn't helping. Treat yourself as if you're someone you care about.

*Impostor syndrome is a paradox. Others believe in you;
you don't believe in yourself, yet you believe yourself
instead of them. If you doubt yourself, shouldn't you
also doubt your judgment of yourself?*

**—ADAM GRANT**

Stephen King once commented that he'd nailed all his rejection letters to a wall and that he'd soon need a railroad spike. Dr. Seuss was rejected by twenty-seven publishers. Agatha Christie encountered five years of continual rejection. Thomas Edison got fired. Henry Ford failed in business. Oprah Winfrey was called "unfit for TV." The average millionaire has failed seventeen times.

Again, it's easy to look at the successful people and assume it was easy. But you don't know what they went through. Got fifty "Nos"? Get through them fast because it only takes one "Yes." The world didn't end. Let it be okay, and then so will you. That first rejection will make you want to crumble. You don't know how to handle it. But if you've been rejected 358 times, number 359 is no big deal.

It takes a special person to look at rejection and say, "Yes, please, may I have another!" Go into anything that scares you with your eyes open, head up, and keep putting one foot in front of the other. You're either all in or you're all out.

*Once more into the fray
Into the last good fight I'll ever know.
Live or die on this day
Live or die on this day . . .*

**—LIAM NEESON (AS JOHN OTTWAY)
IN *THE GREY***

Remember that you have something special to offer that's your unique fingerprint—something only you can do in the exact way you do it. Find out what that is and focus on that. With any one skill, you will always find someone else who is better. But the chances that this person is better in all of your skill sets is slim. Thus, *only you* offer the full skills profile you offer.

Imagine you're a manager at a bank. You will always find better bankers and better managers. But very few will be better bankers *and* managers in the exact same way. And suppose you're expertly trained in customer service. There will be even fewer who are better in all three areas. This is called "skill stacking."

Many managers, in hiring roles over people, don't often realize that it is far more useful to hire the right *person*, who's coachable and trainable (but isn't necessarily fully developed), than it is to hire someone who looks great on paper and knows everything but cannot adapt or learn.

In other words, you could hire someone who is an expert in only one area, or you could hire someone who is slightly less skilled in that one area (but still great) yet perhaps offers three or four other skills. Your return on investing in that person will always yield greater results because they add more ingredients to the pot.

Don't get caught up in analyzing outcomes. And don't confuse your skills with your value. Skills can be developed and will add to the uniqueness of your fingerprint. But knowing your uniqueness requires that you fully explore your life. Remember, you've got to put yourself out there. Stop worrying about other people. Worrying and caring are two different things.

You don't know their situation beyond your assumptions of it. All you know is Michael has a nice car. You don't know how much debt he's in because of it. What do you really know about most people's lives beyond a social media post? Maybe Michael is miserable. In most cases, things are not how they seem. Again, you assume. You also don't know how their story plays out.

I've known many people going through some grisly life events, including abuse, addiction, divorce, and even life-threatening medical conditions. Look at their social media profiles and you'd think they're living in bliss as they smile atop a mountain or practice yoga in a dewy meadow at sunrise as they travel the world. Many people would be jealous of their extraordinary life. Yet I knew them, in that moment, to be greatly suffering.

That person you think is so successful is working sixteen hours per day. From social media, it seems like they make a lot of money. But maybe late, crazy hours at work are putting a strain on their relationship. Maybe they're close to bankruptcy. Do you think they will broadcast that struggle? Maybe you wouldn't want that life. Again, stop paying attention to that stuff; you just don't know.

Besides, what in you is hurt by their success? The part of you that feels like you're not enough. Is that what someone who is confident would think? Would someone who is mighty think that way?

Be happy for others' successes. Be grateful for what you already have. You can't see this, but you're probably living someone else's dream. Someone in the world would change circumstances with you in a heartbeat.

Do you know someone who is better than you at something? Great! Learn. Again, you don't know what they went through to get there. And you don't know where you're going or what you're capable of. Let's see how your story plays out.

Simply decide that you're done comparing.

*Comparison is the thief of joy.*

**—ATTRIBUTED TO THEODORE ROOSEVELT**

Like pushing away from the wall when learning to swim as a child, it takes courage to venture into the unknown and resist the urge to rush back and cling to safety. Those who stay glued to the wall will spend life wondering what it was like away from it, and they'll never learn to swim.

I have never worked with someone who didn't fail—not in business, wellness, academia, or life. The difference is that successful people make adjustments, let it go, and move on; that's it. Again, failing doesn't make you a failure.

So what makes someone, an "ordinary" person, decide one day to change big? Eventually, they realize they need to stop feeding the cycle of mistake, guilt, and complete derailment before starting again and again. They accept a mistake. *They drop it.*

Often, it's not the mistake that derails you. It's what you do after that. It's not the brownie; it's the ten brownies after that when you're eating your guilt. Make your mistake, observe what happened, and try again with unlimited redos.

Are you stuck waiting for just the right set of circumstances to be ready to change? A good question to ask yourself is, "What would have to happen for me to say, 'I'm ready *today*'?" What information do you need to make that decision? Nothing. Analyzing is stalling. You will procrastinate and justify every reason that keeps you stuck. Don't listen to that. You will never mitigate risk well enough to be comfortable. Stop seeking comfort in guarantees; there are none. Trust that you will do what you need to do when you need to do it.

In business, you learn things you will only learn by being *in* business, not just planning to be in business. What seems like endless preparations can only take you so far.

The unsuccessful will always come up with reasons why something won't work. Do you think successful people exercise when the weather is bad? Yes, but you'll notice they're the only ones doing it. The only people in the gym during bad weather, or holidays, are the regulars, and that's because they're regular. They choose purpose over pleasure.

One day while I was working, it began to snow. My first thought was *I wonder if the gym will close early.* I called, and sure enough, they were closing early that afternoon. I rearranged my schedule and made it happen.

When I arrived, I noticed only familiar faces: the people who also "made it happen."

Most clients would have thrown up their hands and said, "Well, I guess I can't exercise today." *That's* how you know what your mindset is and isn't—when your first thought is "*How* do I do this?" and not "*Should* I do this." Look for all the reasons to do something, not all the reasons not to.

When you become uncomfortable, you're on the verge of a breakthrough. Remember that feelings aren't facts, and that the resistance you feel is your mind's natural inclination to cling to safety. To the mind, failure is like death—proof you're *not* the person you're hellbent on becoming. Most people stop too soon. They go 90 percent of the way, then turn back.

Let it be okay, and keep swimming.

*I said to my soul, be still, and wait*
*without hope*
*For hope would be hope for the wrong*
*thing; wait without love*
*For love would be love of the wrong*
*thing; there is yet faith*
*But the faith and the love and the hope*
*are all in the waiting.*
*Wait without thought, for you are not*
*ready for thought:*
*So the darkness shall be the light, and*
*the stillness the dancing.*

**—T.S. ELIOT, FROM "EAST COKER"**

# CHAPTER EIGHT

# Breaking Old Habits:

## *The Essentials*

*Complexity causes suffering if it's uncontrolled. . . .*
*Take a balloon and blow it up beyond its tolerance,*
*and it's going to blow out at the weakest point.*

**—JORDAN PETERSON**

**Lessons from Near Death:**

*Nothing will change unless you do. No program or guru will change you. There is no "system" or series of steps that aren't someone's opinions about what works. Change is about being aware and using that awareness in the million daily microdecisions you make about priorities.*

## CREATE CLEAR BOUNDARIES

It's helpful to realize there are certain things common amongst people who have made big changes in their lives, and they might aid you.

If these practices are not present, you may find change an uphill battle and fall back into old habits.

The following recommendations can help you create a way of thinking about your life as you draw a line in the sand—as you explore a new baseline and determine what works for you. Each of these recommendations serves as guideposts aimed at helping you keep things simpler as you "trim the fat" from your life.

First, know yourself. If you're regularly living beyond your capacity to handle it, you will break. What's sometimes perceived as mental problems is actually just a person trying to create a life for themselves that works. Their inability to do that, and the resulting stress, is manifested in their behaviors.

Most people, regardless of life circumstances, fail to set any boundaries for themselves (in terms of how they choose to spend their energy). "Boundaries" refers to knowing (and understanding) your limits, mental and physical, and setting parameters within which you can live. You may lack the ability to say no to others and thus take on more responsibilities than you have capacity. This has both mental and physical consequences. Be honest with yourself about what you can and can't do physically and mentally, and accept that not everyone will like it.

Find your flow—a balance whereby you can be productive but present, with the ability to make high-quality decisions without overextending yourself. Overextension "involves seeing more to do than one can actually accomplish and feeling able to accomplish more than what conditions allow," according to "flow" expert Mihaly Csikszentmihalyi.

I've worked with many clients who wanted to simplify their lives but didn't know how to say no to people when they were overextended (especially to family members). Listen to your body. If you're at your best, you'll be better for it. And you'll be better able to help others. Not wanting to help because you don't feel well is different than not wanting to help because you don't care. You just don't want to disappoint because you're worried about how your boundary will affect others' perceptions of you.

But, again, you can never control that. You're still the same you, regardless.

"Boundaries" refers not only to setting clear limits with others but setting clear limits within yourself. Don't check your email twenty times per day. Most likely, your work email can wait for work, and your personal email is not that important. Don't let the last thing you do before going to sleep or the first thing you do when you wake up involve looking at something on a screen.

Start to make different choices with your energy. Know how you work best. I know, for example, I get sucked into watching live music or animal videos on my phone. If it's something I enjoy or something that adds to my life experience, it *may* well be worth my time, but there's an appropriate time and place for it. There is also a thin line separating something like that and something that soon becomes a problem. Again, know yourself. In my case, I removed the app from my main screen so it's not always staring me in the face. But you must know your weak areas—your time drainers.

Or, as an introvert, I'm exhausted by large crowds. A trip with a big group to an amusement park would not be an enjoyable time for me, especially if I don't know the group well. I prefer peace and solitude in nature. Others may not understand this or even like it, but I know how *I* function, which is different from how *they* function, which is okay. I give them permission not to like it. But our friendship would not be improved by me going to the park, especially if I'm pressured to go or I'm not feeling well. And if we're true friends, it won't be hindered by me not going, either. It should make no difference.

If friendships have no room for honesty, then they aren't friendships. Be honest with yourself and others. If someone takes issue, their motivations are self-serving.

Perhaps this same friend who invited me dislikes the beach and the ocean and declines *my* invitation. He shouldn't feel obligated and doesn't need a reason. I enjoy the beach and the ocean very much and find great beauty in anything related, but we are different people, and that's okay.

It doesn't mean we can't be friends. Some people prefer chocolate ice cream, and other people prefer vanilla. Personalities are like fingerprints.

Give other people the space to be free because you care about them. Respect them for it. Allow others to be their best. Extend yourself this same courtesy.

Don't let your emotions get involved. Don't be influenced by guilt or vulnerability. You can only do what you can do. Let the rest go.

You will encounter people in your life who don't like you no matter what you do. Accept that. Being agreeable won't get anyone to like *you*, only what you did because they gained something from it.

Again, create boundaries and give others permission not to like it. You must take the oxygen first. Then, you help others.

## FOCUS ON THE ESSENTIALS

*When the time is upon you, start,*
*and the pressure will be off.*

**—YOGI BHAJAN**

Are you focusing on the essentials of change, or are you lost in endless preparations (stalling)? Yes, you can start to change without having it all figured out. Start today with one single step. Then take another, and then another. Keep putting one foot in front of the other, and soon you'll be running.

Often accompanying the feeling of being overextended and overwhelmingly busy is disorganization. You may often, with the best of intentions, set your sights on downsizing, decluttering, or organizing the mess. What you're really saying when you say "I'm busy" is that you feel you have lost control, and coming home to a clean house and organized drawers, files, and inboxes might help you feel you have regained control of the busyness.

And, with those intentions, you focus on getting organized . . . and you'll start tomorrow. Time passes, and after many tomorrows, nothing changes. You continue to slog through the to-do list.

I've had clients who've read seemingly every organizational book, listened to every podcast, or even hired an organization guru, and without fail, once the busyness of mundane life returns, following the temporary boost of motivation, their best efforts fall by the wayside.

You could read every book or listen to every guru, but still, here you are. So why is there no change?

Without changing the way you function at your core, and unless you can see your life and make decisions—sometimes big, scary decisions—that reflect self-awareness, you'll always end up back where you started, wondering how you got there.

## SO, WHAT'S ESSENTIAL?

There are two types of tasks: fixed and flexible. Fixed tasks include appointments such as the dentist or work. No expert in the world is going to help you find more time in a dentist appointment. It takes as long as it takes. If your schedule is filled with fixed tasks, a big decision may be needed to reduce your mass (more on that later).

Most often, people think every task is fixed. Everything's a priority, and they're emotionally attached to them.

First, bring yourself to even. In other words, get your head out from under the water to breathe, and then you can focus on your stroke. You're not going to start very well in the negative; it's got to be from zero, or even.

You may need to start fresh and realize it will take practice, so give yourself some grace and allow unlimited do-overs. If you mess up, adjust and move on. Take one day (or more), set an intentional MO (modus operandi or method of operation) for that day, and execute. You're not going to implement new habits successfully if you've still got to deal with all the accumulation. Use this day to go through the stack of mail, the email inbox, the kids' rooms, the boxes in the attic, or the sock drawer—whatever's been sitting for you. Pay the bills, clean your filing system, and do the laundry. Delete all your emails, or file the ones you need to keep into folders.

Of course, the disorganization always comes back unless you change other things, but start there.

If you wake up one day and say, "I'm ready!" but have no MO (written intent, or schedule, for the day), it's going to fizzle out soon thereafter. It's like weight loss: without looking at the root cause or having a plan, change will only last as long as the motivation and excitement does, which isn't long. This is otherwise known as "yo-yo dieting."

You've started fresh before, but you never addressed the root cause or implemented planned action, even with good intentions. We'll get to the habits, but first, set aside a specific day to take care of the stuff that's piled up.

Ask yourself, in any situation, "What's essential?" If you're starting a business, is printing cards essential before you start communicating with customers or begin income-producing activity? No. Don't get lost in the minutiae. There's a time and place for that stuff. Stay on the critical path. The most essential thing is what's absolutely necessary to stay afloat and on the critical path to making money. Do you need business cards if you have no customers? Do you need them in order to make money? No. Make money *first*. Until you have something, you have nothing. Until you're actually in business and receiving payment for a product or service, all you have is an idea.

Most people have a limited budget when starting a business. And during the beginning stages, they aren't making money. So, when you open those doors, the clock starts, and the countdown begins until it's unsustainable. Make money and spend as little as possible in the meantime. You can get fancy embroidered shirts later.

If you're cleaning your home, is it essential to clean that spare room every week—the one no one is allowed to enter? No. Only clean items and rooms that are dirty. "Cluttered" and "dirty" are two different things. Keep the clutter away, and only clean the items that are used, *not* because it's your (too-frequent) cleaning ritual.

If you're overextended now, is it essential to get two more dogs? Is it best for *them*? Is it essential to gossip at work? Is it essential to have a home that's twice the size you need? It's a waste of resources, and it's a lot of upkeep. Is it essential to pack for every weather possibility before your trip, or will it suffice to check the weather and figure that if the unexpected happens, you'll survive?

You may choose to do or not do any of these things, but each one has implications in your life. With each decision about what's essential, you decide each is worth the cost. Just because you want something doesn't make it essential.

Organization isn't something you sometimes do; it's continuous. It's a lifestyle and a personality. If you haven't needed a copy of a bill in over a year, shred it. You should not have cable bills from five years ago. There's not going to be an issue with October's payment from that time, especially if it went through. It's just taking up space. The only papers you might need for longer are tax documents. But with those, you don't need to view them regularly, so store them elsewhere.

If it's not necessary to keep, it's necessary not to keep it.

Is it essential to be on social media every hour? Every fifteen minutes? Or your email? Very little is that important. Don't let it run your life. Again, boundaries. Check no more than once per day, and be careful not to become addicted to the mind-numbing feed, and post consciously. No one cares about your latest gym selfie or where and what you ate for lunch. In extreme cases, remove the app until you have more practice in mindful nonattachment. If it's not helping you, it's hurting you. If it's not adding to your life, it's detracting from it.

Doing things in the moment is an easy win. In other words, when you get the mail, don't throw it into the stack on the counter. Open it and handle the bills right then and there, using a phone or app. Don't just take off your shoes at the door and fling your jacket on the couch. Take off your shoes and put them in the closet, every time. It's those small actions (like not putting your shoes away) that cause the overwhelming accumulation that you procrastinate dealing with.

Always put things back where you got them. It takes no time and prevents accumulation. As simple as this may seem, a lot of people just aren't doing this.

After you eat something, wash the dishes, every time. Don't let them pile up.

When you check emails, delete, respond, or toss them into an archive folder. Never leave them in the inbox. Be succinct in your email responses (but warm), and get to the point (but stop signing emails with "Regards"). Most people read an email and let it sit and accumulate.

These tasks take seconds but reflect a lifestyle. In other words, your entire lifestyle may be an added weight to your daily experience, and you may not realize the extent. You'll be amazed how much of a difference doing things in the moment makes. Most tasks don't take as long as you think. You can do a lot in five minutes. Time yourself. Try it. The accumulation of tasks creates feelings of being overwhelmed and causes procrastination. The resulting dread, along with poor daily habits that keep your energy low, destroys motivation. The disorganization may not be because you're lazy; it's that you have poor habits or low energy as a result of those habits.

## GUARD YOUR ENERGY

Take care of the high-focus stuff first—the highest priorities—when you still have the energy. It's easier to put something off if you don't have the energy. If you have a big goal but "never have time" for it, do that first; chip away at it each day. Show up. Otherwise, it's easy to get stuck in waiting for the "right time" if something is too overwhelming to tackle at once.

It's okay to be the tortoise and not the hare. Get up every day and do what you can do that day, in the moment. Keep putting one foot in front of the other. Accept that there will always be stuff on the to-do list left undone. But each day is a decision about what's important. Make it consciously. Don't wing it.

Mornings are critical because they set the tone for the day. That doesn't mean you should jump out of bed and dive into email or a meeting. That means you start the morning in the "right" mental space and prioritize your energy. Gurus are quick to tell you to get up super early—to drink a special tea, exercise, or follow their plan, because it works for them. That's all great, but figure out what works for you. It's important to know how *you* work best in terms of your energy.

Your day must be deliberate. Live *that* day, not the day before or the day after. If you don't meet a rigid expectation, you may feel anxious for not getting it done. So there has to be some detachment and flexibility. Give yourself permission to simply do what you can.

Plan your day as needed, but don't feel like a failure if you don't finish everything. Nothing is more important than your daily experience. It's not a to-do list; it's just being deliberate about your day, doing everything you can do, and letting the rest go. Prioritizing your energy is important because motivation waxes and wanes from hour to hour.

Many tools can help simplify your life—electronic calendars, apps, and organizational programs—but none will make a difference if you don't address the root cause of your disorganization (in your daily habits).

There is no one right way to be organized, and there is no magic. The key is "trimming the fat" of your day, implementing solid habits, and detaching (emotionally) from the rest. As you develop new habits, you'll notice things become easier. My inbox, shoe rack, and sink are (mostly) always clean. I have a method whereby my day is streamlined and wasted time minimized. This is not to say organization is about working efficiently all the time for the sake of productivity as if everything else were time wasted. Watching the sunset isn't wasted time. Again, it's about trimming the fat and prioritizing what's important.

When your day builds mass from disorganization and choices you don't realize you're making, you're giving these things too much importance. Start now, and write down your ideal day—your ideal daily schedule, or MO. Work backward from there. You have something written to look at, and you can make critical decisions to help you get there.

First, it will be trial and error. You might try several scheduling tools that don't work. I, for example, eventually settled on an electronic calendar I can access from anywhere. I color-code it (red for important, fixed appointments), and what I don't accomplish (low priorities) I simply click and drag to a day that looks like I might be freer. If I don't accomplish it then either, it's no big deal. I don't beat myself up over it. Just trim the fat.

Organizational gurus will all have methods or tools. Some will work, and some won't. Mindfulness gurus may "live in the moment" and thus don't need a calendar, but what's going to work for you? You can be mindful and still find something that helps—a routine, schedule, or itinerary. It's a safe bet that even a mindfulness guru still has to plan trips to the dentist or pay an electricity bill. You just don't want the fixed tasks to take over your life when everything becomes fixed.

You've got to zoom out and take a hard look at your way of living. Part of guarding your energy involves nonattachment to the to-do list. Intellectually, you know it never ends, but every reaction, thought, and behavior is a rush through each moment to cross off the next task on a list of endless tasks. *Everything* seems important. Everything is a crisis as you list the reasons why you can let go only after today's important tasks are completed.

If you don't start the day off in the right state of mind or with a good MO, you don't live life; life lives you. If you sleep poorly, eat and sleep poorly, wake up late, mismanage your time, etc., your energy level and motivation will drop, and this drop only perpetuates the state of low energy. In other words, you eat, sleep, and do things that keep your energy low, and your energy (and motivation) is so low that you keep doing those things that keep your energy low.

And motivated people in good mental states live well because they're living well enough to keep themselves in those states. Again, you choose how you show up in the world. *You* control your energy. Even when they encounter adversity, people who live in those positive energy cycles are able to bounce back: *I'm going to get through this. I'm so grateful for my family's support.* People who live in bad energy cycles become victims yet again: *I should've known this would happen. It figures. Nothing good ever happens to me.*

I noticed this phenomenon, too. On slow days I had less energy than on busy days, which can be counterintuitive. When I was busy, I tended to be on a roll. I was in the flow, and my energy enabled me to do things that kept my energy high. This is "change momentum." When you eat well and exercise, you feel better, and when you feel better, you're more likely to eat well and exercise.

So, why are you not doing the things you know will help you to be at your best? What are those things?

Part of staying in that good mental state, creating boundaries, and guarding your energy is knowing what relationships are good for you or not. What will you allow?

Most conversations are just random streams of thoughts, or venting. This doesn't mean it's not okay to "shoot the breeze," but know, in that moment, if it's worth the cost. Is that conversation essential? What did listening to an endless work drama do to your energy? Did it pull you in to become lost in it?

Part of being a guardian of your energy means that you don't allow tasks or things to dictate your life experience. Remember, the to-do list will never end, and sacrificing a good mental state now will not help you tomorrow. Work always expands to fill your capacity to handle it.

## NEVER MULTITASK

Watch your mental real estate.

You can't do anything well if you're focused on everything. You can't possibly handle all things at precisely the same time. If you have firm boundaries and know yourself and your energy, you will work how you work best.

If you ask most people, multitasking is generally considered a great skill; it litters almost every job posting out there as a must-have. But when people say "multitasking," they either don't fully understand it, or most often what they mean is the ability to "pivot." And there's a huge distinction between the two.

I'm referring to the big things. Indeed, there will be some degree of multitasking when you're folding laundry and chatting with your spouse. But don't treat multitasking as if it's something to strive for on a daily basis and something you've got plastered all over your resume as a source of pride. Multitasking is a great way to do many things poorly. You simply overtax your mind with too great a cognitive load, so you can't focus on doing any one thing well.

Pivoting, however, is the ability to immerse your complete focus on one thing at a time but with the ability to change directions quickly, as needed. *This* is a great skill. Most people work best in short spurts. Focusing exclusively on one thing ensures maximal attention and focus, and pivoting quickly to something else that utilizes different areas of the brain ensures the mind stays fresh.

The surest sign you're on the path to becoming overwhelmed as a bystander in your own life is when your day consists of endless multitasking. You're never quite here because you're *there*—in the past or future. Checking your email during a conference call is multitasking. Checking your email for a brief period and then having a short, laser-focused conference call is pivoting. You *can* be present in both instances.

You will accomplish far more pivoting than you will multitasking. Again, know your energy. The mind is simply not able to concentrate on something for eight hours straight, like when you burned the midnight oil on school nights cramming for exams. That information will not be retained.

Short spurts are required to stay on task longer, paradoxically, because you've allowed for recovery. Working memory must be available to string periods of focus together. And it requires energy that's usually not available, especially when the mind is noisy.

Think of a computer. If a computer utilizes too much memory on too many tasks at once, such as having too many windows open while you're running an update, the computer will become sluggish, unresponsive, and may even freeze. It doesn't have enough energy to focus on everything you're asking it to do. It can normally handle all these tasks individually, but not all at once.

When you try to force learning that isn't sticky or easily recalled—like when an instructor throws tons of information at you in block text (otherwise known as "death by PowerPoint")—you *will* lose focus. An instructor may understand a topic but not how the brain embeds information. They don't understand how to pace their teachings.

Anyone can relay information, but few can teach it. What's the point of learning if not for long-term recall? In a process called "chunking," information is spaced into digestible bites that resonate or create emotional connections. This makes learning sticky. Then, learners should practice actually doing what they learned to embed that information.

Every day is a test of what your mind can process in a given moment. If you overload it, it shuts down and reverts back to what's a habit for you.

## REDUCE YOUR MASS (DECISION POINTS)

*A quiet and modest life brings more joy than a pursuit of success bound with constant unrest.*

### —ALBERT EINSTEIN

Many people think they're the victims of circumstance when, in actuality, they've just made a series of bad decisions.

Becoming overwhelmingly busy is usually not something you intend. It's a gradual massing of all you've accumulated in your life with the sum total of everything you need to do to keep that going—the implications and unforeseen burdens of years of choices.

"Wow, how'd I get *here*?!" a client often says. Like a snowball rolling downhill, your life gradually gets bigger and bigger as it picks up mass, and with it, the large snowball increases its speed. Soon you can't see a way to overcome it, and all you can do is get out of the way.

When you're not guarding your energy, it's easy to accumulate mass. To you, everything you accumulate has value because you can't see otherwise. And then you must work to retain this accumulation. Because you're in your bubble, you're unable to see life outside it.

Ask someone overwhelmed by this mass how they can simplify life to allow for more time; they won't know. Mostly, they will vent about their circumstances but change nothing. But, again, if you're putting your energy toward what you *can't* do, you'll have no energy for what you can.

This mass is composed of individual decision points. Your entire life is made of them. From the moment you wake up, you start making decisions. Every human being has the same number of hours in a day. What they do with those hours is a matter of many small decisions.

Assume a billionaire executive woke up one day as you, living your life. What decisions do you think they would make differently?

Decisions are either active or reactive. Will this decision help you, or will it take your time for something that makes no difference? Was *that* decision worth the cost?

As a student, a decision point might be the choice to study or not. As a parent, it might be helping a child with his or her homework. Or you might make a decision to leave your current job.

Decision points are powered by motivation (or lack thereof) to change. Any time you make a decision, it's because you wanted to do that thing more than you didn't. And when you're out of energy—when your working memory is burdened by life's noise—there will be little energy left for an active, quality decision. So you'll turn on the television or pick up your phone because it's mindless; it's distracting. Again, your low energy will keep your energy low. You will always do what feels soothing in the moment.

So, what can you do?

You're going to have to make some key decisions to change things. Most of these decisions are going to be outside your comfort zone. Decisions about real change reside there. Real change takes courage. Sometimes you will need to make big, even scary choices. This might mean moving to a different state, quitting a job, or rearranging lifestyles. But unless you're making decisions that help you, you're making decisions that don't.

That's a key decision point: the first one, made of sheer determination in a low-energy state, despite your pain and desire to stick with what's familiar, where you decide to break free from the cycle.

You have to want the change more than you want the habit. That's why many people have to hit rock bottom before changing; whatever that bad habit provides, even if just numbness, is hard to break away from. But you first have to see it. Most people never get to that point because they're busy reacting to the last thing that happened.

Do you work best in the morning or at night? Do you focus best in short spurts? How much sleep do you require? What foods help you feel best? How do you stay organized? What would make your life simpler?

Why aren't you doing these things? What would have to happen for you to start doing these things? Without mentioning what you can't do, what *can* you do?

You can put yourself in the best possible situation with the best possible energy.

Turn off your phone alerts, decide to check your emails no more than twice per day, and take the time-wasters off your phone. Take the unhealthy food out of the house. Pack gym clothes for work. Don't watch television late at night. Go to bed earlier. Do it. If you slip up, do it again.

Write out your ideal day. Move toward it.

Don't rely on willpower. Willpower comes and goes. You can't eat a pint of ice cream if it's not there. You're not going to magically teach yourself to hate it. Even the gurus enjoy it, so what are they doing to help themselves? It's not magic. You're only as strong as your weakest moment, so make choices that support how you work and don't *force* how you work. You won't be perfect, but start making decisions that will help you. Examine your areas of struggle and address those. Write them down.

It's important to maximize your state of being so you arrive at decision points prepared and ready to make decisions that are aligned with your new mental state.

Change is *not* nonacceptance. You can accept where you are on an emotional level but still work to change it. Acceptance doesn't mean you sit back and do nothing.

I once had a client who made a courageous decision. He knew that to change his situation, he would have to arrive at a decision in his best, clearest state. He mulled over the choices for months, unsure if he was ready to leave a job that, although familiar, was no longer aligned with him.

He always knew, from the beginning, what decision he wanted to make. He just had to give himself the permission to make it. Ultimately, he decided to move to a different state and embark on an entirely new career journey.

You can make the best decision *now*. That goes for the big decisions and the small ones. But the reason you feel stuck is because you make decisions that keep you that way.

What have you really done to change things? Change might mean selling items, changing jobs, moving, or starting new relationships (or letting some go). But it always means making choices that are best for you as someone who loves yourself, has boundaries, and knows how you work best.

That's all your life situation is right now—a sum total of a series of decisions you made from one moment to the next, of pleasure or purpose. Some things in life you truly can't control, but you can always control your responses to them—your choices.

## BE MIGHTY

A good, confident leader always does more listening than talking. Truly confident people don't feel compelled to make specific impressions. They know who they are; there's a calmness there. Arrogant people, however, are constantly working to prove something.

*Intend* to do everything you do. People can feel this. Stop apologizing to people for taking up space. Carry yourself as someone worthy of respect. When your energy reflects your fear, you're not attractive to people, and their responses to you will confirm your fears and drive more of them. Attractive people (in terms of their energy) generally encounter more favorable situations that align with who they are in a given moment.

A confident person is deliberate in their actions. They intend to do and say all that they do. And they're intentional in how they choose to use their energy or not. Each choice is a conscious, confident decision about when to expend and when to save this precious energy. They have boundaries and accept that some people will take issue with them.

It never occurs to someone who's confident that they're not enough.

A prominent therapist I once knew described her husband as a man who commanded respect—a man who inspired others, and when speaking, others listened. She called him "mighty." That resonated with me.

She said that as they were dating, whatever his weaknesses, it never occurred to him that he wasn't "enough." She meant that he was confident, and his confidence had less to do with any particular behavior; it was more about a way of being—an aura. If he was broke, short, or balding, it wouldn't make a bit of difference to him. And that made him more attractive.

I paused. That was the key. It was simple yet profound. It simply never occurred to him that he wasn't enough. *That's* confidence. Shortcomings? What shortcomings? You can identify areas for improvement without seeing them as weaknesses or reasons you're incomplete.

"Confident" is not arrogant, cocky, or conceited. "Cocky" is a misguided feeling of "better than." It's tied to the value of others. "Confident," on the other hand, comes from a place of self-love and purpose.

By focusing on your strengths, you will build confidence. Then you can branch out into other things to improve upon your weaknesses. Confidence is knowing how you work best and not being threatened by your weaknesses. Weaknesses aren't shortcomings; they're opportunities.

Want a kid who thinks he's terrible at reading to learn to read? Focus on something else he's good at and allow him to build his confidence. Then, read.

Every human being is insecure about one thing or another, but confidence is the willingness to say, "I'm going to make the intentional decision to be enough, right now, and let the cards fall where they may. I may not know *this,* but I know I have the ability to know it."

You can be confident in your not knowing something. You can be confident in a weakness. Having a weakness or blind spot doesn't make you weak. Own it. How can you know something if you haven't been exposed to it? Learn it. Ask questions. Decide to be confident in your learning.

It's incredible what a simple decision will do. The rest is just noise. Some things you know, and others you don't. Your value transcends any of those things in which you lack confidence.

Look people in the eye when you talk to them, as if you were someone worth paying attention to. Again, we all feel like frauds at some point or another. But that discomfort is associated with venturing away from what's familiar. If you don't feel like a fraud, you aren't stretching. Own it; people can sense how you feel about yourself.

If you're introverted, own it. It's *not* owning it that drives the negative self-talk—the talk that is full of doubt and just makes you more withdrawn. Many introverts are fine when speaking to one person, but not to groups. Groups are judging. They're faceless. When speaking to the faceless, the interaction is sterile, and you become lost in your thoughts of judging. Instead, always speak as if you're speaking to one person. Look at them. Know that they're just people. Once you stop worrying, you're free. You must put yourself out there.

Impressions shape experiences. Even unconsciously, people notice two things about you right away: your warmth and confidence (which is perceived as competence). They will instantly develop feelings based on that interaction, and ultimately you, that often reflect how you feel about yourself.

Warmth is often missed. Particularly in a work setting, I've known many very competent people that still created problems because they triggered defensiveness in others. They were, of course, unaware.

If you're confident *and* warm, you're going to more easily connect with people. Again, few will remember what you say, but they will always remember how you make them feel.

## SLOW DOWN

When you speak to someone, speak clearly and firmly. Most importantly, *slow down.* When you make the conscious decision to slow down in your life and your behaviors, your energy will reflect that.

One prominent characteristic of someone who's not confident is nervousness, rapid speech, mumbling, and tripping over words. When you slow yourself in a deliberate way, your thinking will often match your behaviors.

*Intend* to say that. Intend to walk the way you walk and shake hands the way you shake hands. When you don't know something, say it deliberately. Intend to say it.

Allow this confidence to be clear in your presence. Shake hands firmly. You're the reason for your confidence, not your titles or credentials. And it has nothing to do with what you know or don't know. This person is going to know you're confident because it will show in all that you do. And if you consciously slow down, you're going to communicate more effectively, with confidence.

*You need nothing* from an interaction because you're already enough.

If you don't feel confident right now, *be* that person who is confident. Don't listen to the internal whispers telling you otherwise. This isn't the same as being someone you're not. You're *not* the person who is timid or afraid. You're more yourself when you remove the fear that controls you.

Being yourself is not something you have to do; it's something you allow.

Again, if you're introverted, own it. If you're quiet, own it. If you have a stutter, own it. You don't need approval or permission to be this way. You don't need validation.

Nervous before a big speech? That's okay. Don't berate yourself for it. Don't resist it. Feel it fully. Embrace it. Laugh at it. It is what it is. It's your body reacting to a situation. Confidence is not resisting the fact that you're not confident. It's not berating yourself for being nervous or thinking you shouldn't be. It's being confident in your nervousness. *Own it.* Once you let go, those feelings will dissolve.

Every time you catch yourself in a state of feeling sorry for yourself, immediately stop in your tracks and drop that negative thought. Drop it before the commentary starts. That's a good place to begin.

If you feed negative self-talk with energy, it grows. And you'll know it's happening because your emotions will remind you of it.

If it doesn't help, it hurts. If it's not necessary to say, it's necessary not to say it. Vocalizing negativity, especially when there's no way to change the situation, only adds to the negativity. Complaining never helps anything, and, for most people, it's a habit they don't realize.

While you may not immediately stop the hardwired physical manifestation of an emotional reaction, like nerves or sweating, if you can merely notice it, you can drop the commentary before it runs away with your energy.

*Decide* not to be nervous. It does nothing to help you. They—your boss, an interviewer, or a celebrity—are just people. If you don't speak to people like peers, they won't treat you like one. Simply decide not to be nervous for that reason; you don't need any other. Most stakes are pretty low. Just be a person and speak to others as people. You know more than them about something, and they know more than you; you complement each other. No one is better or worse, despite ranks or titles; there are just people.

Give yourself a break. Slow down. You got this. But also be patient. You've had these bad habits for a long time, and they may be hardwired.

If you fail, fail properly. Fail like you mean it. *Failing doesn't mean you're a failure*—just the opposite. No one is successful unless they've failed. The question is, can you handle it? Again, you're either all in or you're all out. Own it.

What would a confident person do? They *don't* sit around all day wallowing in self-pity about what went wrong. They don't stew in their own internal dialogue, thinking themselves losers; it doesn't occur to them. They don't think the failure had anything to do with their own lack.

They learn, and they move on.

## KNOW WHAT YOU NEED (TO RECOVER): INTROVERTS AND EXTROVERTS

Introverts aren't always shy, and, no, they aren't always boring. They just find joy in different things. One person's excitement about going to an amusement park is an introvert's exhaustion. They may find just as much excitement in different things, like sitting outside and watching the birds or going on a leisurely bike ride.

Introverts tend to need firm boundaries and derive their energy from within. They tend to become exhausted by social situations, not energized, and prefer fewer conversations. They prefer to expend their energy on their own terms. As guardians, they must be steadfast in managing it.

No, they're not always antisocial. No, they're not always bad leaders. On the contrary, sometimes they make the best leaders because they're generally introspective and regulate their emotions well.

It's important to understand the relationship between being shy, being introverted, and being extroverted. Each is different. Shyness is fear-based. Introverts merely recharge their batteries differently than extroverts. Introverts tend to pull back when their energy is drained. They tend to create their own energy internally by retreating to recharge before emerging once again. Introverts need process time. Or a nap. Recovery is absolutely essential for an introvert, or they will easily surpass their threshold to handle it in any productive way.

Extroverts, on the other hand, are ready for the next adventure. In other words, an introvert is compelled to pull back to replenish their energy in situations where an extrovert is compelled to stay for the same reason.

One is not better than the other; they're just different energy languages, each with strengths. Introverts are more likely to observe before acting. They seem to take a while to "warm up." That's because they usually survey the situation, find their bearings, and become more comfortable over time. In contrast, extroverts tend to act more decisively in social situations and usually fit in well with groups.

Without understanding, it's easy to observe and judge a person if their behavior doesn't match what you might do in the same situation. It's hard to understand if you aren't feeling the same things. Again, it's a different language. But what's common is the need for validation, belonging, and to matter. Because you don't know what's hidden behind a smile.

# CHAPTER NINE

# What's Real

*A little while and I will be gone from among you, whither I cannot tell. From nowhere we come, into nowhere we go. What is life? It is a flash of a firefly in the night. . . . It is the little shadow that runs across the grass and loses itself in the sunset.*

**—CHIEF CROWFOOT**

> **Lessons from Near Death:**
>
> *Cherish relationships that are real. Cherish the beauty in your life. It goes by faster than you think, and it always catches you by surprise. It's a tough pill to swallow to realize you've spent your entire life focused on the wrong things—the things that didn't matter anyway—and it's too late.*

If you knew the exact time of your death, would you think differently? No matter how long you have left in your life, your time becomes more real once a doctor quantifies it. Things become clear in ways they never have before, and you realize which relationships were real.

Remember, the cost of a thing is how much life it takes from you. The first things you lose in life are your relationships; they tend to suffer quietly because they require the one thing you don't have: *time*. There's always more time for them . . . until there's not.

"I love you" is a common expression. We proclaim this to those we will, sometimes, despite the best of intentions, eventually divorce. We are "in love" in absolutely every romantic relationship . . . until we aren't. We "love" ice cream. We "love" a movie. We "love" a shirt.

The person you "love" is a summary on a dating profile that reflects a few common interests: craft beer, "having a good time" or "having fun," and "hanging out with friends." You both like to "go out" sometimes, and other times you like to "stay in." (Is there another option?) You want someone that "keeps your interest"—someone who entertains you.

Clearly, you "know what you want" in a partner. You mentioned that right in your profile. Has anyone ever said, "I guess that counts me out because I only want to have a terrible time"? You check the boxes like grocery lists—items you need off a shelf. But aren't you looking for love? If you find it, how will you know? Is it love if it's conditional?

Your "love" is conditional on your partner aligning with your perceptions and expectations of them. The degree to which that condition is met is proportional to the extent that you're fulfilled and made whole. In this way, your love is about you. It's a dance as each person, smitten, demonstrates their feelings about the other person in ways that bolster each other's feelings about themselves.

"He makes me feel . . ." a young woman says as she begins to describe her new partner. Yes, but why do you love them beyond how *you* feel? Can you explain that love without talking about *yourself*?

"You're so great. Doesn't this feel perfect?" you might say a week into a relationship.

In this way, your happiness is based on the degree that someone fulfills your needs (or not); in most cases, it's not a conscious decision of partnership based on anything you actually *know*.

"Are you in love?" asks a dating show television producer who's built a narrative for the sole purpose of driving ratings.

"They make me feel so amazing, and I've never felt this way before. I can totally see us getting engaged at the end of this," one contestant says on *The Bachelorette* during a time when they're "vibing." They've gone on just one date in a vacuum outside of anything close to real life.

"What's most important to you in a person? What are you looking for?" one contestant asks another.

"Honesty. And someone who can make me laugh." (As if anyone would say anything different.) They are "falling for" that person . . . until they're not.

"How did you feel when Bryson kissed Kendra right after he said he was falling for you?" the host asks a contestant.

"I thought we were in love," the contestant says, sobbing.

"I'm . . . so sorry," the host says as producers fan flames to bump ratings.

How many ways are there to feel about that? It's the drama business. "Are you not entertained?!" shouts Russell Crowe as Maximus, "The Spaniard," in *Gladiator.*

When you make someone an option, you will leave them when they no longer fulfill you, which they can't." You both know so little about the other person, but it doesn't feel that way at the beginning. You think you know what the word "love" means as it flows from you so freely. You can't wait to say it, and later you recount how big a deal it was who said it first.

"I know what I'm doing," you say after a months-long engagement.

"We finish each other's sentences," you both say simultaneously. How cute. Who would've guessed that six months from that moment, you'd be bickering about finances, who's taking the trash out, and why you washed your new red shirt with the whites?

Yep, true love's a bit more mundane than it was when you were finishing each other's sentences.

There is a very thin thread between love and hate. What once felt like a beautiful love soon turns to the most intense hatred as divorce lawyers prepare your case and you troll social media, trying to find anything incriminating on the other person. You once "loved" this person, you said, but you apparently "grew apart," or "fell out of love," or you "want different things." Now it's contempt, and familiarity breeds it. Think things are wonderful? Try living together for a while and see if you're both still starry-eyed.

"Hate" is a strong word, but so is the "love," which you both of course meant at the time. Mostly, you meant that the euphoria felt like love, but it was really infatuation born of the novelty back when both of you were on your best behavior and seemed to fulfill needs.

Anyone who's been through a nasty divorce can tell you that the feeling of hate is also intense. At the time, you can't help but act disgustingly. "They deserved it," you might say in the heat of the moment. Yet your hateful behavior is "not who you really are." You're right about that.

You become unhinged. You become the emotion and act in ways normally thought uncharacteristic as you fight to the death over frivolous items like flowerpots and the fancy wine opener. You want to beat them to a pulp so much that the smallest of things (that you don't care about) become symbolic victories to punish this "person" for being such a demon spawn. Reason rarely factors into it. It's them and their emotions and you and yours, each rambling on about how the other person is nuts.

You can fall into this hate almost as easily and quickly as you fell into love. It's scary how familiar this process is. But this onetime partner is now your enemy, or at least it certainly feels like it. It's not really about right and wrong; you're trying to win, yet there are no winners.

You react outlandishly when threatened, which is often. There's no awareness of the common humanity—the pain in the other person—as both of you inflict upon the other pain that will surely reverberate into your futures.

They try to protect their identity from becoming vulnerable by trying to diminish yours. You do the same. Egregious amounts of time and energy are wasted behaving in ways that don't reflect who you are. You became an endless series of reactions hellbent on winning. You have become a vessel for pain and can only react as the angry internal dialogue rages, rehashing memories of how you've been wronged. And so you spend more and more time. It can only stop when one or the other is present enough to step back from the madness and look at it.

Ordinary people—you, me, your family, friends, and everyone else—are capable of behaving in all sorts of ways normally thought uncharacteristic given just the right circumstances. The heat of the moment fuels reactions that soon run away with you. You simply never know how someone will react in a given situation until you see them in it—even yourself. Otherwise good people do bad things one step at a time.

I can tell you, unequivocally, that I have found myself in several situations that I never dreamed I'd experience, perhaps even some for which I'd judged others earlier in life. In some cases, I learned a great deal more about myself and what was real and not. You can never know until you're actually in a situation. The rest is just speculation.

But regardless of how you feel, it's not love, and it's not hate; it's weather. I know the hate feels real now, but it's not. It's just an emotion. It, too, passes. Weather changes. The tides ebb and flow.

Too many times, I've seen the greatest lovers turn to enemies, and then, decades later, as the clouds pass, the hate dissipates. You can't see it in the moment, in a bubble. *That's* not them, and *that's* not you. Your reaction clouds reality. It's a story that should be taken with a grain of salt.

Maybe they're wrong, or maybe you are. It doesn't matter. You'll never know. Your "love" and "hate" are emotional knee jerks. When the "love" fades and your partner is "not who you thought they were," if you could look beyond the reaction to see their humanity, you would see that no matter how bad it gets and through whatever they say and do, their behavior is just a reaction to a previous reaction, and a long string of them. What will you do? Will *you* react? It comes down to a decision. You're not talking to a person in that moment. And in some ways, they don't know what they're doing.

If you start rationalizing and mulling over what's true (or not) in all this, you will go mad. Truth has nothing to do with it. You can't reason with them. Again, never get into the weeds with someone. If you do, you lose. The moment you participate is the moment you're the same as they are—on that runaway train. You don't need to defend yourself. What are you defending? Who do you think will hear it?

If you want peace, choose peace. Stand there like it doesn't matter. It's hard to react against someone who's not reactive.

Try an experiment. When someone is awful to you—when, ordinarily, you would become emotionally charged—be calm, or even kind. Just try it and watch what they do. Just let them be right. It doesn't make the truth less true.

They may become surprised or even confused. They aren't used to it and don't know how to handle it. It's a decision of energy. Again, people will soon rise or sink to your emotional level.

"But I want to give them a piece of my mind! They're wrong! I can't just let it go!"

Pause. Why not? Part of you thinks you'll make yourself whole or the truth truer by hurting them, or that you'll find some way to rectify the situation. That will never happen, and whatever lesson you think you're teaching them, you're not. You're threatened. You're defensive. You're venting.

Hurt people hurt. If you can't find anything to love, love their humanity. Stop creating a story. Stop creating a problem. There is no problem if you decide there is no problem.

## WHAT MAKES LOVE "UNCONDITIONAL"?

"I love you unconditionally," you say as your partner, child, parent, or sibling basks in that love. But what does that mean? What makes your love so unconditional? Knowing someone? Thinking you know them? Unless, of course, it's "love at first sight."

Or perhaps it's blood (genes)? Unless, of course, there's adoption. So, two people had sex, and one of them birthed you, and because they did that (which is usually nothing they actually did but rather something their *bodies* did), that's love? Every creature on the planet can have offspring. The fact that you were the one that came out of that person is either chance or part of "God's plan." So you love them, in many cases for something they didn't intend or, at the very least, control. And because the same thing happened to your sibling, and thus you share some genes, you love them too?

But what do common genes mean about the essence of a person? Shared history. Familiarity. Diddly. Imagine you meet a long-lost brother or sister. Do you love them? Who is that person? It doesn't matter; you love them.

But adoptive parents can love equally as those who did not adopt. So it's not blood, but a choice? If you choose to love someone, by implication that means there must be something about them you love—something that makes you choose it—or else it's not choice but rather instinct or some sort of obligation or responsibility to a person.

If love is a choice, it's *always* conditional—conditional on that person being exactly who you think they are. You can't love someone you don't know because you wouldn't know who you're loving. Sure, in an esoteric sense you can love the humanity in someone, but that's not what you mean.

Maybe you "love their heart." Your love is conditional on that "heart" being what you perceive it to be. And if the person you love suddenly turns out to be a serial-killer rapist, what, exactly, do you love again? You love who you thought they were.

If your love is "unconditional," it that to say there's nothing this person could do for you to stop loving them. Or, to put it another way, what would have to happen for you to stop loving them? Most people would say nothing . . . until there's something. Imagine your son is this serial killer. What about him do you love? Your shared history? So you love the familiarity. Or it has nothing to do with them, and so it's blood—the fact they have your genes. Obligation or instinct.

What if you discovered that the child you raised was actually the product of your wife's affair? So he's *not* your blood. Do you love him? Of course. It's too late; the loving connection has been forged. It was forged when you thought it was blood, but it's not. So it's either the shared history (the memories), or there's something about him you love, which makes it conditional.

You also love your spouse—*not* blood. You love your adoptive family—*not* blood. So love is not really about blood. Then it's conditional on you knowing them and being accurate in that knowing.

It's a choice you make each day to love *that* person. It could be a choice born of familiarity, obligation (of a role such as a parent loving their child), or, most often, thinking you know someone. After all, who would love a torturer-killer outside of a fuzzy instinct to do so? No one. If your love is instinct, again, it doesn't matter about knowing the person; it's about *you*.

When people use the words "unconditional love," what they are describing is an intensity of a feeling. Lots of divorced couples loved each other "unconditionally" at some point until they reconciled what that means when their perception of a person changed. And until we reconcile what it means to love each other and life, love will always be fleeting.

Love isn't the keeping of scores or resentments. Love is a thousand small kindnesses. It's treating your partner like your best houseguest. It's an expression of your connection to another person. Love is beyond the roles. And it's *conditional* on knowing the essence of a person to the extent you're able to do so. And, like most things in life that are real, knowing something or someone means exploring that knowing. *That's* your purpose in life. Don't wait until it's over to discover that, instead of exploring your life, you were a bystander in it.

## THE MOMENTS IN BETWEEN

I remember walking outside of my office to one of the most breathtaking sunsets. I stopped in my tracks and gazed at the sky. The moon was full with a beautiful glowing ring around it. A few bright stars and some wispy white clouds were scattered over an otherwise crystal-clear sky of dark-blue hues.

As I stood in awe of this breathtaking sight, a coworker walked out of the building with her head down, hypnotized by her phone. That moment burned into my brain—the image of a woman with her head down, checking pictures of her friend's new manicure, oblivious to the most beautiful sight I've ever seen.

Most people enjoy a sunset, but how often do they actually look? You'll give anything to see one more when you're lying in an ICU bed, and you never look at it the same again.

Such moments of joy are what you will long for in the end. You'll give anything to eat one of Mom's Christmas cookies or smell Dad's old work shirt. There's a bittersweetness when you think about those memories; you'd love to experience them again, even for a moment.

Those small joys seemed to slip through your fingers like burnt paper. Most of those joys are hidden in memories triggered by encounters that remind you of something. Maybe it was a smell or a picture. Maybe it was something in a movie or reminiscing with a family member that put you back in that moment.

In her book *Tinkerbell Jerusalem*, Bonnie Kelley Kaback calls these moments "inbetweens." These are profound moments that seem so small and insignificant during everyday busyness. Even now, I look back during the darker times and realize that I may never see my son do something cute like that again, or I'll never experience that smell or sound or touch like that again. The smallest moments—often the most meaningful ones—seem to slip away as we anxiously rush to get through our days and to the next and the next.

Life isn't about happiness; it's about the moment-to-moment experience. Again, *nothing* is more important than your daily experience.

I love the smell of fresh-cut grass; it reminds me of spring. I love cold sheets when you first get into bed. And I have my special place that I go to: there's a gazebo there, a pavilion, willow trees, a bridge overlooking fountains of water that sparkle like diamonds, and lights that shoot out of the middle of the small lake. I'm happiest there, and I'm in awe every time.

I'd like to go there more often . . . but I've been busy. Tomorrow, perhaps.

You can die, or you can live until you die. *You*, and no one else, decide how you do that.


*Life will break you. Nobody can protect you from that, and being alone won't either, for solitude will also break you with its yearning. You have to love. You have to feel. It is the reason you are here on earth. You have to risk your heart. You are here to be swallowed up. And when it happens that you are broken, or betrayed, or left, or hurt, or death brushes near, let yourself sit by an apple tree and listen to the apples falling all around you in heaps, wasting their sweetness. Tell yourself that you tasted as many as you could.*

**—LOUISE ERDRICH**


"Living" isn't necessarily about a bucket list of skydiving or traveling the world—rushing to live after a life half known. It's about the day-to-day. It's about being in a moment, sitting outside on a warm summer day and watching a rabbit family chase each other in the grass. It's about seeing the beauty there. How often do you suppose people just sit on a random Tuesday in awe over something like that? No phone. No talking. Just you, there.

Understand that most of your days will be mundane and unremarkable, but there's beauty everywhere. If you look through a drinking straw into an area of the sky that appears to be blank space, you're actually looking at over ten thousand galaxies and billions of stars—just in that drinking straw. It's impossible to grasp what that means. Everything we see is inside our galaxy alone. We are unfathomably small. And on the timeline, we aren't even a blip.

The end of life always happens on a strangely mundane and ordinary day. It's even anticlimactic and seems to catch most people off guard. You were expecting a parade, perhaps? At least, you expected more than this obituary which certainly has no mention of your titles or roles that meant so much while you were alive. Of course, the end is not something you can adequately prepare for. I mean, who thinks that after brushing their teeth and ordering a pumpkin spice latte that they've only fifteen minutes left? Don't lose sight that *this* moment is all that you own.

Today, at a traffic light, I looked to my left at a woman applying her makeup. I looked to my right at a man texting on his cell phone. A strange feeling enveloped me, and I can't describe it.

One day, your side of the bed will be empty. The night before, you were there, just like thousands of ordinary nights before that. Now, on an ordinary Tuesday, the person you love sleeps alone for the first time. All your stuff is exactly as you left it. Your desk is still messy, and your favorite hat is atop your dresser. Someone you love will go through those things to be donated or sent to the landfill. You love that beat-up hat, but, yes, it was just a thing.

You hoped the world would be shaken after losing you, but it moves on. The woman that cut in line for coffee the day before continues with her life like always, oblivious to the fact that you're gone. She's in line again at your usual place, but you're not there. She doesn't notice.

Today, that same woman will have a terrible meeting at work and buy a new purse on the way home. And she's still a jerk.

*If this is how it ends, maybe it's not so necessary,* you'll think, *to obsess over keeping absolutely every dust particle from the furniture, to check social media every ten minutes, or to insert myself in a workplace drama.* When you're a party to a drama, you become the drama.

If you know when your last day will be, suddenly that latte is extra sweet and the drive to work extra beautiful. That sunset you miss most mornings is always beautiful, but you never used to look at it like *this*. Normally, you're distracted by the slow driver in front of you, the traffic, or a text message. And your worries? What worries? There's no time for that because there are limited tomorrows. And, suddenly, your whole perception of *everything* is skewed, along with your perception of time and the illusion that you have more of it.

After my second cardiac arrest, for which I was already in the hospital after my first, I could feel the darkness close in, but faster. But before it did, there was an incredible pain in my arm from the IV concoction. I contemplated yanking out the IVs on my own. I can't imagine what it would feel like to have my arm explode, but I suspect that was pretty close.

I knew there were things I would no longer do again—things that made me dizzy or risked a broken lead. Some of those things had been tied to my identity for so long. I realized I had two choices: I could choose to wallow in self-pity (which would do nothing to help the situation), or I could choose how I was going to show up. And no matter what I could or couldn't do, I was still "me," and I was alive.

Hospital food became like fine dining, and even the ability to walk without feeling dizzy or light-headed was a treat I'd not take for granted. Like the food, I began to look for the good in everything— every silver lining. I never imagined feeling such deep gratitude for a little hospital ice cream with its tiny wooden spoon.

On the occasion I had five minutes when I felt "normal," that very normality reminded me of the extent to which my entire way of living was dedicated to managing my own ability to function.

Whenever I felt my heart quiver or another wave of dizziness, I'd wait a few seconds until the blood returned. It was a surge of warmth that blanketed me. I was a vampire with a thirst for blood . . . in my brain.

Come to think of it, it appeared hazy outside, my skin was (and is) pale, I did have an immense thirst, or hunger, and I also burned (and still burn) easily in the sunlight . . .

Even now, I feel each time my pacemaker takes over with its strange, robotic beats. After the initial shock of "What the hell is going on in my chest?" diminished, the sensation became strangely comforting because at least I knew it was working, ticking away. But it was hard to get used to, especially at my relatively young age. But every day, I wonder how much time I'll have; it's like a constant game of roulette.

I think about death constantly—not in a morbid way, but in an honest one. I've already tested it twice. How will I go? If not a cardiac arrest, a heart attack? Aneurysm? Blood clot? Cancer? Car accident? Pick your poison.

It was hard to feel like I hadn't lost my personality through it all. This was not how I would normally act. After all, you've got this concept of who you are, but each day I focused on the same small wins: get up, try to function "normally," or at least pretend, and, as soon as possible, retreat to my bed for some always-needed rest. My days as a workhorse were over.

No, it's not fair; that's the brutal indifference of life. It's not about what's fair. Life is about being who you are with the time you have and exploring life as that person. It's about discovering how to do that when each moment is an opportunity *not* to—an opportunity to do what's easy, or entertaining, or pleasurable. But not what's best for *you*.

We're fragile. Life is fragile. It always dumbfounds me how so many can't see this—how they can seemingly throw caution to the wind as if their life (and health) weren't worth more. They take it for granted.

Of course, you can't live afraid all the time, but it's something else to make decisions as if you're invincible. For example, I never quite understood the choice to become a boxer or mixed martial artist. I don't understand literally signing up to be repeatedly hit in the head. The brain (and body) wasn't intended for that. Surely, shaving years off your life for a sport, for entertainment, isn't worth the time you'll miss with your kids.

Every moment I'm dizzy is a reminder of how much I'd taken good health for granted.

One of my waves of dizziness lasted for a year or two, at least, with daily fluctuations in intensity that were somewhat reduced by avoiding certain triggers. I had to be vigilant with how I spent my energy lest I crash again.

With limited energy for the minutiae, you become disinterested in gossip, arguments, or other trivialities. You learn to let certain things go because you only have so much energy, and it's tied up in merely functioning. Every moment is a choice because it has to be. And you have to have boundaries. You don't "feel like" worrying because you can't afford to. It's just not a priority. When the ability to walk to the bathroom without feeling faint is a treat, you aren't going to worry about mowing the lawn or finishing the report at work. Again, worrying and caring are two different things.

I recall many situations in which I became so sick of worrying that I just chose to stop. That's it. I just said, "I don't feel like it anymore." It was that simple. I surrendered to it. It's about giving yourself permission to stop the overanalysis. Worrying helps and changes *nothing*. Remember, boundaries.

The silver lining, I suppose, is that it's easier to be aware of how you spend your energy if your current physical state is a constant reminder of it. It's in times of feeling relatively good, without any major ailments, that you take your "good" feelings of health the most for granted. And it's during such times you're most likely to make decisions that don't help you. You have energy, but it's siphoned into all the mass you've created in your life.

Weather permitting, I often enjoy a bike ride during afternoons or evenings. I did this before my event and am even more grateful to do it after. It provides me a small bit of peace, especially when the dizziness is so bad that I'd do anything to be one of those geese by the pond so I could fly toward all the beauty of that sunset tapestry.

Again, life at the end isn't about completing bucket lists or cramming as much as possible into the shortest time. It's about slowing down to see the things you didn't before—the small things—and taking them in.

On a quiet, beautiful summer afternoon, while on one of my bike rides, I returned to a small group of broken gravestones on a hill, obscured by the trees on the edge of farmland. I jumped over a ditch and carried my bike up through the overgrowth and into the trees to investigate.

The area had long been forgotten. Many of the stones were broken and covered with all that remained—a mere stump of stone barely protruding from the ground amongst the branches and leaves. If not for the three or four that stood erect, I wouldn't have known the graves existed at all.

There were maybe ten stones or remnants of them. Upon one, dated 1840, I could make out the words "Do not worry about me, for I'll be waiting for thee."

Two other stones also drew my attention. One was unbroken but very small. The other was very large but broken at its base and sunken into the earth, the top portion of the stone leaning against an adjacent tree.

The first, the small one, belonged to a thirty-year-old man who died in 1880. I was surprised how young he was when he died.

It was common in that time for families or communities to be buried together on their own land. This is more common in Southern, rural areas of the United States from Virginia and through the Carolinas. Drive through some of the older towns, and you'll notice small groups of stones along the road, many that are old and forgotten. It's remarkable to imagine these lands and what they were like—the beauty—years ago before.

What struck me most about this stone was that he was my age (at the time), and I had just knocked on death's door myself. A couple hundred years from now, this could be *me*; this could be *my* stone, for a young man's unexpected demise.

I had knocked on death's door, and had I not been revived, there may well have been someone standing over my lost gravestone, should I be so lucky, wondering about this long-forgotten young man resting quietly under the rustling trees. That's me right there.

And, suddenly, as I stood there, I felt small. That work drama was small. The ding on my car was small. It's all small.

I imagined what might have happened to him. Did he get sick? An accident? I wondered about him as a person. Maybe he was married with kids or divorced. He probably had worries, and fears, and goals, and dreams. Maybe he was deeply in love. I couldn't imagine how much the landscape had changed since then. After all, just around the bend was a freshly repaved road not far from a new housing development. And, perhaps soon, all traces he was here at all will be gone.

Perhaps he was popular. Perhaps what made him popular was the trendy act of tucking his pants inside his stockings. Perhaps he was popular because he was an avid croquet player. It really made me step back and look at what's trendy, now, as it passes. Trends seem to mean so much to people.

But it didn't matter. All that remained of this man was a small dusty stone, a life summarized as a dash between dates. And there's no one left to mourn him. Anyone that ever knew him is gone. They, too, are here amongst the trees. It's so quiet here.

All his worries, fears, hopes, and dreams are gone with him. Did they still happen? What makes something real? Again, look through a drinking straw into the sky and know that you're looking at the incomprehensible, even in the darkness. Then think about your problems.

I removed a few items from my backpack, placing them on the ground beside the base of the broken stone. With some warm water and a cloth, I cleaned its surface, reading what was inscribed. This one was 1878. I took my brush and gently scrubbed the broken base to remove any dirt and debris.

I picked up the stone and laid it flat. It was deceptively heavy, almost unbearably. I washed off the rest of the dirt and the numerous tiny spiders. I began to mix a small bit of concrete on a piece of cardboard, experimenting with different types of coloring I sprinkled into the mix.

I used my brush to ensure that the concrete paste completely coated every jagged nook of each corresponding surface. Then, with a burst of strength, I lifted the stone atop its base and held it firmly in place. Because it was so top-heavy and the grave itself sunken, I used the strongest pieces of various nearby sticks to help prop it up until the concrete mixture hardened.

I cleaned a few other stones, then left. Every time I pass, I check to see if it's still standing. At least then a long-forgotten young man was a thought in someone's mind. It's what we all want—to matter.

*We shall not cease from exploration*
*And the end of all our exploring*
*Will be to arrive where we started*
*And know the place for the first time.*

**—T.S. ELIOT, FROM "LITTLE GIDDING"**

# CHAPTER TEN

# In Hindsight

*The Moving Finger writes; and, having writ,*
*Moves on: nor all thy Piety nor Wit*
*Shall lure it back to cancel half a Line,*
*Nor all thy Tears wash out a Word of it.*

**—OMAR KHAYYÁM**

> **Lessons from Near Death:**
>
> *Accept that who you are is beyond your full knowing and that your life is about exploration. Most people spend a lifetime trying to become what they already are as the world makes them into everyone else.*

It's Monday morning—the normal, the routine, the humdrum. You started to dread it the moment the weekend started. Your alarm goes off, that incessant shrill that marks the start of another workday—the beat of the never-ending drum. After the eightieth mashing of your finger into the snooze button, it's time to get up.

You clumsily stagger out of bed with all the joyous aches and pains of a bad back. Maybe you walk into a wall. Your breath could kill, and you've got a major case of bedhead.

You brush your teeth like always and spend an hour working to get your hair and makeup as close to perfection as possible before coordinating your outfit and posing in the mirror. You change clothes several times until you find something that makes you feel somewhat okay before you put on sunglasses the size of dinner plates and head out the door.

You recheck your makeup in the rearview mirror or, in halfway-reasonable traffic with music blaring, take another selfie for a few "likes." You probably skipped breakfast, or perhaps you grabbed something on the way.

After you curse the morning traffic, a deluge of fast, uncomfortable thoughts enter your mind about all the things you have to do that day: the dry cleaners, the bank, picking up the kids . . . and can you believe what Tonya said to you yesterday? You roll your eyes. You'll have to deal with *that* today, too. But meetings, emails, and a new client account take up what's left of the morning.

The weekend seems an agonizing eternity away. It taunts you. You desperately long for it, wishing time would go faster and faster to get you to the relief of another weekend that, of course, goes by in a flash when compared to the week.

You're supposed to actually live your life on weekends, but they're always a bit anticlimactic as you end up sitting, lost in your phone, or binge-watching shows about murder. You feel guilty you didn't use that time better. You always think you will, you promise as much, and you plan it, but, strangely, you never do. You're just too tired.

Friday feels fantastic, but you're exhausted. You want to rest this weekend, but you don't want to sleep it away, and, of course, there's so much to do. Saturday is the day you're supposed to "live," but it's gone in a flash. On Sunday, the building dread for the week is heightened. The countdown to Monday, which started the moment you got off work on Friday, seems to speed up as you cling to what's left of your Sunday, which feels like the last one for a long, long time.

Another Monday arrives. You pass a coworker in the hall.

"How are you?" someone says at the office.

"Good, you?" you say with your mind elsewhere.

"Eh, it's Monday," your coworker says.

The week is a blur, just like all the weeks before it and all the weeks after. But there's a strange comfort in the familiarity of the routine.

You swear if you make it until retirement, you'll finally live. You'll travel and sip margaritas on some tropical beach. You'll finally do all the things you dreamed of doing that you waited so long to actually do. And you'll trade every moment of your best years on the gamble that you'll be well enough to enjoy it, and have enough wherewithal to do so.

Maybe you think that's an exaggeration for you. But your prime years are gone. Or maybe most of your years are gone. Congrats, you can finally enjoy life for the first time at age eighty. Now, if you could just pry off that ankle bracelet and sneak out of the home . . .

If you knew that your life would end only six months into retirement, how would that change your perspective of how you spent your prime years? You'll think of all the years you worked and wonder if your life could have been simpler. You'll think about what was worth it (or not). It was an everyday life, sure, but how many years were spent maintaining life's mass or in keeping up with the Joneses (who are now gone)? What was essential? Now things look clearer, and, for most, it's the first time you have this clarity.

Imagine you've been retired for a week. Haven't you heard? Your old position is filled already, by some twenty-something. And just think, you built that role from scratch! You did so much for that company. You meant to travel and take time off, you really did, but you were "ambitious."

Now you can enjoy that highly anticipated stress-free living you've heard about, which consists of more television than you'd imagined. You don't quite know what to do with yourself. You don't feel like traveling, anyway, because you're tired. There's always tomorrow . . .

For twenty-five years, an old colleague, Joyce, worked the same job before suddenly passing away. One week prior, she attended an open enrollment meeting to discuss her benefits and retirement changes, that long-awaited retirement just a few years away.

The day before Joyce died, I passed her in the hall. I had recently returned from a short trip, and we soon found ourselves in a conversation about all the places to which we wanted to travel.

"I would love to go to Hawaii," she said. "I've never been. My goal is to go after I retire." She was sixty at the time.

I always think of that conversation.

The following day I, like every employee in the company, noticed one of those form letters in my company email inbox: "It's with a heavy heart that I must inform you that one of our team members, Joyce Donald, has passed away. Our thoughts and prayers go out to her family during this difficult time."

For most people, it was the first (and last) time they would see her name.

She was gone, and so were her tomorrows. And her passport was still empty, each blank page a stinging reminder of an experience unlived.

These types of letters are well intended, I'm sure. Perhaps even appropriate. Yet there's always a contrived, generic quality to them as if, on some template, "Joyce" replaced "[insert name of dead person here]." Over the last few years, I've received about a half dozen of these emails upon my arrival in the mornings. Minus a few shifts here and there, each was nearly the same. They seemed to blend together.

"To the Liberty Healthcare Family," one began, a typical form letter. *Family?* I thought. *Is that what we are?*

"With a heavy heart," the letter continued. *Whose heart is heavy? The person writing those words? What does that really mean?* I wondered. How can they care, beyond empathy, without knowing that person? When you watch the evening news and hear of a stranger's death, which happens every day, is your heart "heavy"?

I imagined other employees simultaneously skimming the email, breathing a reactive sigh to sad news that barely permeated their bubble, then clicking "Delete." They'd already forgotten her name.

"Oh, that's sad news. So what are you doing for lunch?" said a coworker in the break room. The local employees (those around Joyce's immediate work area) were shocked, but not because they were deeply aggrieved. Most didn't know her aside from the pleasantries—the how-are-yous. Rather, they were upset because the shock hit "close to home."

Reactive people don't know they're reactive; that's part of the reactivity. The extent to which most people are "shocked" or awakened is proportional to the extent an event permeates their bubble to disrupt them—to pull them into the moment.

"I just saw her last Tuesday!" the "anguished" said of Joyce's passing. This coworker really didn't think that was the last time she'd see her.

"A colleague of mine passed away this morning," I heard her say to a friend on the phone later that day.

"I'm so sorry!" her friend probably said, not realizing the coworkers' interactions were no more than an occasional passing in the hallway.

"It's tough," she lamented, feeling a bolstered sense of self driven by all the condolences. "I don't know how I'll go on without my dear friend, but I'll trudge through somehow. God, I miss Jean, my angel."

"Joyce, you mean?"

"Yeah, that's what I meant."

Joyce's life is now summed up in a half-inch-long dash between dates chiseled on a stone somewhere—and who knows where. Only a select few, and none at work, would know. We can have genuine relationships in the workplace, but in most cases, the people we spend the most time with care more about the role than the person.

Joyce's title wasn't on the stone. Nor were her credentials, the fancy MBA, or mention of the nice car.

It was quiet.

It's hard to think of your whole life summarized by a half-inch dash—all the experiences and memories.

Now and again, a client will say something that profoundly affects me. I often speak with clients in varying degrees of awareness, but one conversation resonated. This woman had been very much in love once and married for thirty years.

"It's rare to have that kind of love," she said. "It didn't matter what we did. I remember sitting there next to him after watching an absolutely terrible movie. I remember looking at him and thinking, consciously, about how much I loved him. He also thought the movie was awful. But I just stared at him as we sat quietly next to the open window, after thirty years together, and I said, 'I don't care what we watch or do, good or bad, I'm just so happy to be in your presence.' He died the next day. I'm so glad I said that."

> To love life, to love it even
> when you have no stomach for it
> and everything you've held dear
> crumbles like burnt paper in your hands,
> your throat filled with the silt of it.
> When grief sits with you, its tropical heat
> thickening the air, heavy as water
> more fit for gills than lungs;
> when grief weights you like your own flesh
> only more of it, an obesity of grief,
> you think, How can a body withstand this?
> Then you hold life like a face
> between your palms, a plain face,
> no charming smile, no violet eyes,
> and you say, yes, I will take you,
> I will love you, again.

**—ELLEN BASS, "THE THING IS"**

Time is funny; you only see it with any halfway-real perspective after it's passed. Don't forget that it always seems slow in the moment until it's gone. Your workday, workweek, and meetings seem to drag on as you long for the weekend that passes by in an instant.

You stare at the clock until the next thing you have to do, the next thing, and the next. It all seems to go by at a snail's pace, but one day you'll think differently when you look back; it catches you by surprise. Remember, at the end of life, no one ever says, "Whew, that life went by way too slow!"

As you get older, time seems to pick up speed. Birthdays blend together. At some point, if it hasn't already come, there will be more days behind you than ahead. Imagine if you knew the exact day you could say that.

Time might seem especially slow day to day after thirty years married to the same person as their little daily quirks drive you nuts. But, one day, when they're gone, you'll miss those things. You'll think back with the bittersweet nostalgia of a life once had.

You'll see a picture of your younger self with your family. That's a different life, it seems—almost a different person. It's a fuzzy, distant memory now.

You see your partner every day, but there will come a time when you struggle to remember. You try so hard, but the memory is fleeting as it's carried away by a breeze. You once knew each and every curve of her entire body. And now, for the life of you, you can't remember her face. That's the saddest part—the memories you can't miss because they're already gone.

Sometimes I have flashes of my first dog, my high school prom, or I'll hear a song that triggers a memory of a special moment. Or maybe it's that one beautiful sunset at my special place by the pond, with all its smells and sounds. For a while, those memories are just flashes as they begin to disappear. You'll do anything to picture them again. But you can't.

I remember an interview Oprah Winfrey once had on her network with Betty White. When asked if the then-ninety-three-year-old White had any major regrets in life, she stated that she had just one.

"I spent a whole year, wasted a whole year that Allen and I could have had together, saying 'No, I wouldn't marry him. No, I won't. No,

I won't leave California. No, I won't move to New York.' It was a whole year we could have had together," she said about her husband, Allen, who died of stomach cancer in 1981.

Stop waiting. You wait in lines. You wait for the weekend. You wait for the paycheck. You wait to meet someone. You wait to *be* someone. You wait for next year. You wait for tomorrow. You wait for the end of the day. You wait for circumstances. You wait to see your friends and family. You wait to be happy.

You wait for the end of life; you just don't know it.

You're too busy to call your friend to wish them a happy birthday. You're too busy to do everything you intend to do as the birds chirp and the sun sets.

You're here for a blink. Love the cute little things your kids do even though they exhaust you and drive you nuts; you'll miss those things. Love that kids are still dreamers; don't take that from them. Next time your son runs water through his hair, puts stirring sticks between his fingers, and transforms into Wolverine in line at a Starbucks, as my son did, cherish that moment because it will soon be a memory and, too soon, one that fades. You'll miss that, too.

No amount of tears will change the past. Learn from it and move on. It only takes a moment to change. Again, real change can take courage. It can take grit. It's not something that happens to you; it happens *because* of you.

Stop carrying the pain of your past—pain from breakups, rejections, or other losses—and stop thinking those stories are unique and insurmountable. We all break hearts and have ours broken. We will lose those we love, and friends will come and go. Our parents will not be around forever; cherish your time with them.

You're the company you keep, and if your company is little more than fleeting, hollow relationships constrained by constant worries about approval, that's all you'll have.

You will never be younger than you are right *now,* so stop telling others you feel old. Just enjoy your age and the experience that comes with it. Explore what's beautiful in your life. If you're healthy, have family around you, a warm home, and it's a sunny day, your life is pretty great.

We are quick to criticize but slow to compliment. The worst thing to do is have a kindness that you keep inside. We ought to build each other up, not break each other down. Next time you like someone's dress or they did a great job with something, give them a compliment, even a stranger. *Especially* a stranger. You don't know what someone is going through; make their day. You don't know where the experience will lead.

There will never, ever be someone like you again. Don't take that for granted.

Don't take the people you love for granted because there will never be someone like them again, either. And they'll be gone in a flash on some ordinary day—a day too soon at a time you won't be ready. It's a call we all get. We know this, peripherally. But it's profound to really grasp the knowledge that you'll never see them again. Not ever. And no amount of time you ever had with them would've been enough. What was once an ordinary dinner at a new restaurant turns into "He would've loved this meal—this place. He would've ordered *that* . . ."

What was once only a rare, occasional loss when you were young becomes a part of your life as you get older. You say goodbye to people you desperately try to hold on to as they slip through your fingers. You intended to see them next month, and now you can't.

When I woke up this morning, I had a realization; I thought about my parents. I wondered how many Christmases I would have left with them. Say I had four. *Four.* That doesn't seem like very many. Think about all the memories and beauty over the years, and *there's only four left*, then three, two, and one. What if it's *one* Christmas? What if we've already had our last one together?

Something happens when you quantify it. Hearing the clock's tick somehow makes time more real, more precious, and life fragile. It's easier to know how precious it is if you've four left instead of some indefinite mystery number when you're still living on the to-do list that never ends. Not knowing how much time is left allows us to live in the assumption there's so much more of it.

My parents are already about a decade older than my grandfather was when he passed. He died when I was nine, as did my grandmother on my father's side. I wonder what it would have been like to know all of my grandparents. I didn't, and when I was young, I was too immature and lost in meaninglessness to realize it.

I thought of my grandmother. One day she was fine, and three weeks later, she was gone. And she was about my parents' age now.

We somehow think we have so many more opportunities to be with them. We assume that we do . . . until we don't. Then, after that last Christmas, we look at it wishing we'd cherished it more; we would have been more present that last time. We never know when it's the last Christmas, or birthday, or sunset.

I recently noticed an obituary that was listed without a picture. It said, "David R. Wells passed away October 29 in Fairfield." That's it? *That's* his life? His value? And if only one person attends his funeral? Or none? Is that a measure of his mark on this world?

No, he was so much more than that. He was more than his work. He was more than his resume.

Of the top regrets of the dying is the wish they hadn't worked so hard—that they'd cherished the "in betweens."

Let us imagine eternity represented by a long string that wraps around the entire planet and never stops. Although incomprehensible, let's imagine that your lifespan on this string of time that stretches around the globe is just a centimeter. It's about as long as a dash between dates. *That's* your life on a gravestone.

Be the guardian of your energy. Stop saying you're too busy to live during the dash. Time is slipping away as I write this. It seems to speed up as it slips away. I always marvel at the passage of time. Just yesterday, I was at school, dreaming of life ahead. And in the blink of an eye, decades have passed, faster as they go.

When you see a sunset so beautiful that you lose yourself in it, breathe deeply to take that in. It's just as beautiful no matter how much money you make and no matter what kind of car you drive. The sky doesn't care. How many more will you have?

On one normal, ordinary day after one of those sunsets, the tide will go out, and you with it. Go knowing your life was more than half known.

You are not a noun; you are a verb.


*The morning wind spreads its fresh smell. We must get up and take that in, that wind that lets us live. Breathe before it's gone.*

**—RUMI**

CPSIA information can be obtained
at www.ICGtesting.com
Printed in the USA
LVHW111949290322
714728LV00002B/34